"*Relational Apologetics* is a rare book. It avoids the two extremes of painting apologetics as a purely
tionship to evangelism alto
Johnson Chair of Science ar
Southern Evangelical Semi

MW00584394

"As Paul encouraged the Thessalonian believers, so Sherrard encourages us to go about our life and work in a way that makes the gospel believable and defendable." —**James Flanagan**, PhD, president, Luther Rice Seminary

"Well-written, fast-paced, easy-to-read, [and] insightful in a wide variety of other ways. . . . Recommended." —**Gary R. Habermas**, distinguished research professor and chair, department of philosophy, Liberty University and Theological Seminary

"A full-orbed and mature reflection on what it means to be an engaged follower of Christ in a radically skeptical age." —**Craig J. Hazen**, PhD, founder and director of the MA program in Christian apologetics, Biola University, and author of the novel *Five Sacred Crossings*

"*Relational Apologetics* is a much-needed work that I heartily endorse. . . . [It] draws on the conviction, exemplified in the lives of Jesus and the apostles, that apologetics, as pre-evangelism, is most effective when it is done relationally." —**D. Scott Henderson**, PhD, associate professor of philosophy and apologetics, Luther Rice University & Seminary

"It is good to have a concise means of sharing truth in an age of pluralism such as ours. Sherrard's *Relational Apologetics* achieves this goal in a humble fashion. Here is an approach to defending one's faith that is altogether new and refreshing while at the same time biblical and timeless." —**Dylan Higgins**, teacher, and author of The Emblem and the Lantern series

"Michael Sherrard combines a profound Christian mind with a deep love for people. Throughout the pages of this book, you will see a winsome defense of Christian theism that engages rather than repels. In a 'gotcha'

culture obsessed with caustic sound bites, Sherrard challenges Christians to do better—to love not only the truth but the ones who need it most."
—**Scott Klusendorf**, president of Life Training Institute, and author of *The Case for Life*

"*Relational Apologetics* is essential reading for all Christians who desire to effectively and faithfully engage the unbelievers in their lives." —**David H. Leonard**, PhD, assistant professor of philosophy and apologetics at Luther Rice University, and founder of Calling and Culture (www.callingandculture .com)

"This is more than an 'answers' book. Yes, Sherrard provides answers. But he also includes content related to the all-important quality of being the kind of person people will hear. . . . If you are looking for a book that will guide you into becoming a better witness for Christ, your search is over."
—**Michael R. Licona**, PhD, associate professor in theology, Houston Baptist University

"I wish every believer would read this book. *Relational Apologetics* challenges, convicts, and equips us to lovingly reach out to people with the gospel and to live as the kind of humble and gracious apologists Jesus wants us to be." —**Sean McDowell**, PhD, Biola University professor, speaker, and author

"Evangelism simply is *Relational Apologetics*. Sherrard's new book clearly explains the Christian approach to sharing your hope in Jesus. It's a must-read for everyone who loves God and people." —**Andy Steiger**, director of Apologetics Canada

"Michael Sherrard has a pastoral heart and an evidential mind. He understands the critical role our personal lives have in communicating the gospel and he's written a book to help others grasp the importance of our relationships when making the case for what we believe." —**J. Warner Wallace**, cold-case detective, and author of *Cold-Case Christianity* and *God's Crime Scene*

relational apologetics

DEFENDING THE
CHRISTIAN
FAITH WITH
HOLINESS
RESPECT
AND **TRUTH**

2ND EDITION

michael c. sherrard

Kregel
Publications

Relational Apologetics: Defending the Christian Faith with Holiness, Respect, and Truth
© 2012, 2015 by Michael C. Sherrard

Published by Kregel Publications, a division of Kregel, Inc., 2450 Oak Industrial Dr. NE, Grand Rapids, MI 49505.

Library of Congress Cataloging-in-Publication Data
Sherrard, Michael C. , 1979-
   Relational apologetics : defending the Christian faith with holiness, respect, and truth / Michael C. Sherrard.—Second Edition.
   pages   cm
1. Witness bearing (Christianity) 2. Interpersonal relations—Religious aspects—Christianity. 3. Apologetics. I. Title.
BV4520.S453   2015   239—dc23   2015000418

ISBN: 978-0-8254-4233-9

Printed in the United States of America
15 16 17 18 19 20 21 22 23 24 / 5 4 3 2 1

To the love of my life—my beautiful bride, Terri—
my precious gift, the mother and teacher of my children,
and my partner in preparing them and others to impact
our world for Jesus Christ

Contents

Part Four / Where You Go

Preface

*As it is written, "How beautiful are the feet
of those who preach the good news!"*
—ROMANS 10:15

Beautiful Feet

Feet are repulsive. They are not objects of beauty. Yet there is nothing more beautiful than the feet of those who preach the good news of Jesus Christ. But while it is quite easy to say that the feet of those who preach the gospel are beautiful, these must be our feet as well. We must proclaim the hope found in Jesus. We all must be evangelists.

Sharing the gospel is not easy in our day. The world does not tolerate exclusive beliefs. We will be hated for preaching that it is only in Jesus that people can be saved. We will be called judgmental, arrogant bigots. We may lose our jobs, our friends, and even be alienated from our family members. Some may even lose their lives. But because there is nothing greater than knowing our Lord, we must sacrifice ourselves in love so that others may have the chance to know Him. That is why this book was written: to help you be able to defend your hope in Jesus and lead others to Him.

Now, I am not a genius. There is much yet for me to learn. This book will not answer every question. I may even be wrong at some point. A great fear I have in writing is that my view on something may change, and then I will have in permanent form something I think is wrong. But using that kind of reasoning, I might later change my view back to what it originally was, and then I would be no worse off. Anyway, omniscience is not in the cards for any of us, so the best we can do is write with a limited amount of knowledge.

Why This Book Was Written

This book grew out of my students' desire to know both that Christianity is the "right religion" and how to communicate that truth to others. Many of them had friends who were skeptical of Christianity. They wanted to know how to maintain their relationships with them, while at the same time persuade them to follow Jesus. They were frustrated with not knowing how to answer skeptics' questions and respond to their objections. They were tired of the arguments that always seemed to accompany their talks about God. And, quite frankly, they were fed up with feeling belittled because of their belief in God. I imagine you can relate to this.

My students' desire to know how to defend their faith is a desire that I think most Christians have. It is my desire—one that led me to study religion, philosophy, and apologetics in college. The books I read were great. The lectures I heard were brilliant. Yet most of my students and fellow Christians would not have understood them. Furthermore, defending our faith cannot be reduced to an intellectual exercise. It is a relational experience.

Don't misunderstand me. I firmly support the academic efforts of brilliant scholars who seek to affirm Christianity through the highest levels of scientific and historical research and philosophical argumentation. It is certainly needed and has immense value. Having answers, though, is not enough. Christians need a way to communicate truth, not just collect it. And they need a method of communication that is suitable for the sidewalk and coffee shop, not just the university. Formal debates are good, but they don't work well in your workplace or neighborhood.

Apologetics is a tool for all of us, not just the intellectual elite. Christians need a way to explain to their neighbor who is not a philosopher that absolute truth exists. They need a way to explain to their amateur skeptic classmate why belief in the resurrection is not foolish. Simply, they need a way to leverage difficult and intimidating questions for the gospel. We all must be able to answer how we know that Christianity is true. And we need a method that empowers us to use what we know rather than become paralyzed by what we do not. That is what this book provides.

Relational Apologetics is about how to share and defend your faith, non-scholar to non-scholar.[1] It will not delve deeply into the scientific and philosophical arguments for the existence of God and the validity of Christianity, but it will provide solid, simple, and easily remembered reasons why one should believe in both. It will also teach essential relational skills that are necessary to talk to skeptics and maintain a healthy relationship with them.[2] Healthy relationships combined with a reasonable explanation of a Christian's hope are the best type of apologetic, and they are something that all Christians can do.

What Is Apologetics?

Apologetics is simply a defense or justification for something, but in this context, it is the defense of and evidence for the Christian faith. Christian apologetics is a discipline that uses history, science,

---

1. Even if you are a scholar, it is helpful to learn how to defend your faith in relational, nonacademic settings.
2. Scholar and philosopher Gary Habermas modeled such skills in his friendship with former atheist Anthony Flew. The two had many debates about God and the resurrection of Jesus Christ. Before Flew died, he changed from atheism to Deism (he still had some hang-ups about special revelation), and he credited much of this change to Habermas.

and philosophy to show that God exists and that He has revealed
Himself most fully in Jesus Christ. Its purpose is to strengthen believers' faith and equip them with the tools necessary to explain the
hope within (1 Peter 3:15).

Apologetics is a necessary part of evangelism in our postmodern
world,[3] where many lies obstruct the truth of the gospel: *Truth does
not exist. All religions are the same. The Bible was forged. The resurrection was a fake.* Faithful evangelism requires us to know the cultural barriers that keep Jesus out of our society. And more than know
them, we must be able to remove them (2 Cor. 10:5).

There are various ways to go about this, but *Relational Apologetics*
stresses the importance of your entire life becoming a defense of the
Christian faith and an obstacle-clearing path to Jesus. As good am-
bassadors of our Lord and faithful stewards of the Word of Life, we
must be prepared to engage this world with the gospel and respond
to any challenges. We all must be apologists.

The Value of Apologetics

I often hear that apologetics has no value in evangelism, that all
you need is the gospel. People say that you can't argue someone
into heaven and apologetics has never saved anyone. They are right,
mostly. The gospel is what saves, not apologetics. But people must
hear the gospel to believe it and be saved. If you were to say that
the Chinese language has never saved anyone, you would be right.
But if you are going to preach the gospel in China, you had better
learn Chinese. Good missionaries learn the language and customs of
the people group they are trying to reach. I have never heard a mis-
sionary say, "I don't need to learn Chinese. I've got the gospel." That
would be a ridiculous attitude.

Likewise, as good missionaries, we need words and concepts that

---

3. Another application of apologetics is pastoral. But that is another book waiting to be written.

are suitable to convey the truth of the gospel to our culture. We must learn to speak the language of our time.[4] For example, say you meet a person who does not believe in truth. You tell him that Jesus is the only way to be saved.

"What do you mean . . . *saved*?" he replies. "Saved from what?"

"Sin."

"What's sin?"

"Sin is all the wrong things you have done."

"I don't believe in right and wrong. Truth doesn't exist."

"Yes, it does."

"No, it doesn't."

Do you see how you are speaking a different language? If someone doesn't believe in truth, *sin* is a meaningless word. It is gibberish and the gospel won't be understood. Apologetics helps to create a common language between the skeptic and the believer. By enabling the Christian to explain things like the existence of absolute truth, apologetics allows the gospel to be heard.

An Apologetic Lifestyle

Speaking a different language is one reason people don't hear the gospel. Another one is Christians. We have a reputation for being rude and arrogant hypocrites. Sometimes this accusation is justified. There are many Christians who are hypocrites, and conversations of faith can quickly turn into shouting matches because of us. You know. You may be guilty. However, whether it's because of silence, an

---

4. In times past, one might not have needed apologetics, though it is abundantly clear that apologetics have been part of gospel sharing from the beginning (Acts 17:2–4; 18:4; 2 Cor. 5:11; 10:5; Phil. 1:7; Col. 2:4; 1 Peter 3:15; Jude 3). Particularly in the United States, previous generations grew up immersed in a Christian worldview, a set of beliefs that affirmed things like truth, sin, and a need for forgiveness. The culture spoke our language. But times have changed. The Christian worldview is gone and with it went a suitable language for gospel sharing.

unholy lifestyle, or just plain rudeness, *you* must not be the reason someone doesn't hear the gospel. And therein, again, is the reason for the title of this book.

Relational Apologetics is about your life becoming a defense of the Christian faith. Every relationship you have is an opportunity to connect people to their creator as you display your hope, both in word and deed. Defending your faith is not just about answering questions and "proving" that God exists. It is about showing that He is real by the way you live. It is about demonstrating the power of God through your holiness. And it is about drawing people to Jesus through your kindness.

The best apologetic for Christianity is holy people who speak the gospel with their mouths and show the gospel in every aspect of their lives. Truth has no power when it comes from the mouths of hypocrites. If we are to faithfully defend our hope in Jesus Christ, we must focus as much on who we are and how we talk as we do on what we say.

And so I ask that as you begin reading this book you search yourself. Pray that God will make you a worthy vessel of the gospel. Defending Christianity is a good and noble task, but if all you want to do is win an argument, your heart is not in the right place. Defending your faith is not an act of arrogance. It is an act of love. So pray that God changes your heart as much as your mind as you read.

I pray that if you need to repent of unfaithfulness to the gospel, God will convict you in the pages to come. My prayer is that this book serves you as you seek to be a faithful servant of Christ, committed to speaking truth in love to all you meet. And I trust that because you read this book, you will have a stronger desire, matched with an improved ability, to make much of Jesus Christ and not yourself.

Acknowledgments

It is quite difficult to acknowledge all the people who contributed to the writing of this book. There are many people who have invested in my life. This book is the result of the efforts of so many. Below are the people, though, who have had a direct influence on the writing of this book.

I am forever indebted to my parents, Mike and Susan Sherrard. I can't explain the value of the home you provided for me and Brian and Laura. The riches we have because of your faithfulness to us are immeasurable. Thank you. Above all people, you are the reason this book was able to be written.

I am indebted to the students at Skipstone Academy for inspiring me to write this book. Your passion for sharing your faith is what moved me to write.

I am indebted to Jonathan Cooper for helping me actually write. I both hate and love your honesty. "Get it down and then get it good." Your words freed me to write.

I am indebted to Dylan Higgins, who never was too busy to listen to what I wrote. Without your ear, I would never have finished. Your friendship is priceless.

I am indebted to Joanna Jury and Barbara Toth, who read this book over and over again. They took a mess and made it neat.

I am indebted to Rick Schenker and Blake Anderson for their support and leadership at Ratio Christi. This book would not have made its way into many hands without you.

And lastly, I am indebted to my wife. I am indebted for much more than this book, but the way you love me and our kids gives me the foundation to serve others. Thank you.

Part One

Who You Are

Chapter One

Holiness

The greatest single cause of atheism in the world today is Christians who acknowledge Jesus with their lips and walk out the door and deny him by their lifestyle. That is what an unbelieving world simply finds unbelievable.
—BRENNAN MANNING

The Obstacle of Hypocrisy

There are many obstacles to coming to Christ. For many it is not an easy road. There are family issues, intellectual objections, pain, unanswered questions, guilt, pride, and so forth. You do not need to be another obstacle for someone. Sadly, though, the hypocrisy of Christians is a reason—and a fair one—that people reject Christ.

I often hear pastors respond to the claim that there is too much hypocrisy in the church by laughing and saying, "Sure, the church is full of hypocrites, and what a good place for a hypocrite to be."

Usually the pastor then adds that there is always room for one more, the idea being that all people are hypocrites at some level. But this should not be tolerated. Hypocrisy is a sin, a serious sin. It is a sin that Jesus addressed. And it is a sin that the church needs to destroy, not joke about.

It is true that people don't always live up to the standard they set for their lives, and it is true that the one who hates hypocrisy likely has moments of hypocrisy himself. There is one difference, though, between the Christian hypocrite and the non-Christian hypocrite. The Christian hypocrite claims to know God and His will. This is no small claim. It is the grandest of all claims.

Knowing God and His will should affect how a person lives. It's hard to imagine that someone could meet God and not be changed. What message is sent by people who claim to know God but live in direct contradiction to His commands? I think it sends the message that they are charlatans and liars. I think it makes the gospel look false and devoid of power. I think it shows that they do not really believe the words they preach. I think it shows that they do not know God.

The fact is, your life either draws people to Christ or it pushes them away. Whether you like it or not, you represent Jesus. Your words and actions have gospel implications, and your life is intended to be a light that guides people to Christ (Matt. 5:13–16). However, when your life is not in step with the gospel, your hypocrisy casts a shadow of doubt over the life-changing message of the cross (Gal. 2:14). For when you, a believer in Jesus Christ, are no different from the nonbelievers to whom you speak, the gospel appears to be nothing more than a fairy tale: a nice story that is without any real power.

If the gospel is to look real to a world that is perishing, you must not look like a fraud. It is for this reason that hypocrisy must be replaced by genuine holiness.

The Objective of Holiness

Christians are commanded to be holy like our God (1 Peter 1:15).[1]
We are to pursue pure and righteous living, free from all sin. Perfection is our aim. This is a daunting task. It is overwhelming to know that our lives are to be holy acts of worship to our God (Rom. 12:1–2). Thankfully, pursuing holiness is not something that we do in our own strength. God is working in us, both to will and to work for His good pleasure, and He will complete the good work He has started in us (Phil. 2:13; 1:6).

Even though God will accomplish His purpose in our lives, namely, our holiness, it is still our responsibility to kill the sin in our lives through the power of the Holy Spirit (Rom. 8:12–13). We must act on the power supplied to us every day and seek to become like Jesus. Holiness is a pursuit in this life, not a destination, and when we stop running the race to become like Christ, we will be overtaken by hypocrisy. This is precisely where many Christians are today.

Many of Christ's followers have traded in the pursuit of holiness for the pretense of holiness. It is much easier to pretend to be holy than it is to pursue a holy life. And the easiest way to fake a holy life is to point out the sin in others instead of searching for the sin in your own life. You likely know someone who does this. You may even do it yourself. But understand that God is no fool, and the ability to spot

---

1. Just to be clear, I need to make the distinction here between positional holiness and personal holiness. Positional holiness is something that true believers possess. It is not something that needs to be sought every day. It is something we receive as a result of our faith and hope in Jesus. Those who place their trust in Jesus for the forgiveness of their sins are acquitted in the heavenly court of all crimes and sins and are set apart and consecrated unto God as a holy person. In that sense, all true Christians are holy (1 Peter 2:9). On the other hand, personal holiness relates to the lifestyle of a Christian. It involves the daily surrender of your will to seek to do God's will. It involves active commitment to live a pure and God-honoring life. From this point on, when I refer to holiness, I am referring to personal holiness.

the sin in others is no sign to Him that you are sinless. Rather, it is likely the sign that you are a hypocrite.

The Nature of Hypocrisy

Christians must be concerned more with their own sin than the sins of others. Jesus explained this while preaching on judgment during the Sermon on the Mount. He said, "Why do you see the speck that is in your brother's eye, but do not notice the log that is in your own eye? . . . You hypocrite, first take the log out of your own eye, and then you will see clearly to take the speck out of your brother's eye" (Matt. 7:3, 5). Here we see that, according to Jesus, hypocrisy is the result of exposing your brother's sin but not your own.

This was perhaps the greatest problem Jesus had with the religious leaders in His day. Jesus routinely called the Pharisees and Sadducees "hypocrites" because they were concerned more with condemnation than self-examination. They exposed the sins of others yet gave little consideration to their own. In fact, many of them did not even consider themselves to be sinners. But Jesus was not fooled. They were, according to Him, whitewashed tombs: something that looked good on the outside, but had death on the inside (Matt. 23:27).

This hypocrisy in the Pharisees stemmed from their misunderstanding of what it meant to be righteous and holy. They presumed upon their status as Jews, God's chosen people, and did not believe that judgment was on them. Therefore, they were not concerned with holiness; they believed God had already made them holy. They misappropriated God's favor and were blinded by an overestimation of their status. This is dangerous. Relying on past actions is the breeding ground for hypocrisy.

This same problem is in the church. Many Christians presume upon God's mercy as they look back to some past prayer they prayed, and they use it as a license to sin as the Pharisees did. They believe they have escaped the penalty of sin, so they continue to sin. But salvation comes through faith, and faith is active. True believers practice righteousness (1 John 3:9–10). They do not vainly cling to a prayer in their distant past and neglect present obedience. They trust in Jesus daily, and their good works show it (Matt. 5:16; James 2:14–26).[2]

A proper understanding of the gospel should cause Christians to actively pursue holiness. It should cause forgiven men and women to hate the sin that sent Jesus to the cross and motivate them to purge it from their lives. The good news of God's mercy and kindness should lead men and women to repentance, not guilt-free sinning. Many Christians misunderstand this and exploit their "saved" status. They rest in their past and become numb to their sin while they judge the rest of the world. They pretend to be holy by showing how others are not. This type of living makes a mockery of Jesus' sacrifice on the cross.

The Holy Apologist

The way to avoid hypocrisy is to seek holiness daily by asking God to search your heart, petitioning Him for forgiveness, and embracing His power for repentance. Clothe yourself in humility. Submit your life to others. Do not think more of yourself than you ought. Understand that every day you must be concerned about examining your own life more than examining others. Ask the Lord to show you the sin that remains and ask Him to forgive you. Then you need to repent. Know that repentance is a practice of the righteous, not something that is only for "pagans." Do not be a hypocritical Pharisee and pretend to be holy by judging other "sinners." Rather, be holy and let the light of your life show the darkness of others' sin.

A daily repentance, turning away from sin and toward Jesus, is perhaps the most important apologetic for God you can have. This

---

2. I do not mean to imply that salvation is the result of works. But those who truly know Christ and have been saved do good works. There can be no assurance of salvation without them. This is one of the major themes of 1 John (2:3–11; 3:4–24; 4:7–21).

is because your life must reflect your message, or your message will appear to be false. But if your message matches your life, you will be a light that is impossible to miss in a dark world.

Know that your personal holiness is a command from God, and it is one that has gospel implications. Your love and mercy toward others is evidence that God exists. Your changed life demonstrates the power of the gospel. Your life matters. It is not only the words of pastors and theologians that display the evidence and glory of God. It is you.

As we consider how to defend our faith, let us first make sure that our faith has changed us. Let us first ask ourselves if we truly hope in Christ, and then examine our lives to see if we are living as if we hope in Him. If our lives contradict our message, our defense of it will only further harden the hearts of skeptics against God. Therefore, let your life be an apologetic even before your words are.[3]

---

3. This does not mean that you should never directly expose the sin in another person. Christians are called to expose sin. However, such confrontation must only happen on the foundation of self-examination and personal repentance. Only Christians who are committed to removing their own sin are qualified to help others remove theirs.

Chapter Two

Humility

It was pride that changed angels into devils;
it is humility that makes men as angels.
—SAINT AUGUSTINE

The Limits of Our Knowledge

You don't know everything. Nobody knows everything. Not even your condescending, skeptical coworker or classmate who has made you feel intellectually inferior for believing in God. So fear not. A lack of knowledge puts you in the same boat as everyone else. We all have our limitations. It is good and comforting to know this.

Realizing that you are not responsible to know every answer to every question a skeptic might ask should be a huge relief. It is not a burden the Christian need carry. Many of us never attempt to defend our faith because we fear not having an answer. Hear me: it is just fine not to have an answer. There is absolutely no shame in saying, "I don't know. You raise an interesting question." Understand that a person's eternity is not dependent on your knowledge.

Not only is it a relief for you to understand that "I don't know" is an option, others will appreciate your honesty in admitting your lack of knowledge. We like humble people, and in a day of glory-seeking pontificators, your honesty and humility will be greatly appreciated. It shows people that you aren't out to win at all costs. It shows people that you value them more than the argument. It shows that you respect them enough to concede to a good point and allow them to look smart. Because, let's be honest, one of the reasons we get angry in arguments is because we feel the other person doesn't respect us and is making us look dumb for believing what we do. So when you can say, "I don't know. Good point," it shows the other person that although you disagree with him, you don't think he is an idiot. Such humility goes a long way toward developing healthy conversation and lasting relationships, which are both more likely to produce fruit than firing facts back and forth.

A Credible Lack of Knowledge

Admitting that you don't know everything also protects your credibility. This may seem backward because we usually think credibility is found in having answers. However, respect and credibility are lost faster by offering wrong answers to questions in the attempt to win an argument than by humbly admitting there are some things you do not know. The ability to concede in an argument will guard your reputation and allow you to maintain the respect of the other person despite your lack of knowledge. It is important to understand that much of what a person thinks about what you say is affected by what they think about you.

I learned this truth as a result of having an ongoing friendship with a person who didn't believe in Jesus. My skeptic friend and I frequently had conversations about faith, but I remember one day better than others because it changed the nature of our conversations. We were engaged in a typical back-and-forth argument, and there came a point in our conversation when I didn't have a good answer to one of his points. I hated it. First, I am competitive, and beyond that, I just like to be right. So I had to practice the humility of shutting up and saying, "Good point. Let me think about that."

My friend's countenance softened, and his expression was worth the price of my humility. It was as if a burden was taken from him. His tone softened and the rest of our talk was very pleasant. In that moment, my humility allowed him to feel respected, to know that I was not out to get him, and to know that I recognized his intelligence. Backing down was the best thing I did in that conversation.

The Power of Humility

By reflecting on this situation and my own natural hatred of backing down, I have come to understand one of the reasons we don't admit it when we know we have no answer.[1] We think that if we lose one argument, we lose the entire battle, and our friend's soul will be lost forever. We believe the lie that our one moment of yielding will be all the proof the skeptic needs to maintain his rejection of God. But this is simply not true. In fact, our humble "I don't know" can become a bridge that enables us to lead someone to Christ.

Humility disarms. It brings down the other person's defenses. When someone's guard is down they are more likely to see through their emotions and consider what you are saying. Sometimes all it takes is a small crack in the skeptic's intellectual bastion for the light of the gospel to dispel the darkness of unbelief. Humility that disarms and brings respect may be the light that allows someone to see Christ.

I have found that my humility brings out the humility in others, and humility is essential to coming to Christ. The proud do not see God. When I am humble enough to admit that I don't know something, or I am able to admit that the other person has made a good point, it affords them the opportunity to do the same. And then, their

---

1. Pride is most likely the main reason. But I'm sure you didn't need to buy a book to learn that.

humility and lack of defenses make them more open to hear the truth of the gospel and respond to it in a positive manner.

The Humble Apologist

I know that many of us like to think we know everything and some of us actually believe that we do. But this attitude is of no use. It must be thrown away. Pride must be killed before it has a chance to grow into a monster that causes people to reject Christ. Arrogance, self-importance, and smugness have no place in the heart, mind, or conversations of Christ's disciples. Therefore, be diligent in destroying the pride that is likely to surface in conversations about your faith.

Be grateful that the fate of a person's soul is not contingent on your knowledge. Realize that in God's grace and providence you are but a small part of His divine plan in drawing people to Himself. This is not an excuse to be lazy and not expand our knowledge, but it is a crucial understanding to have nonetheless. So start practicing humility in your conversations and do not be afraid to say, "I don't know."

Chapter Three

Readiness

*But in your hearts honor Christ the Lord as holy,
always being prepared to make a defense to anyone
who asks you for a reason for the hope that is in you.*
—1 PETER 3:15

A Call to Readiness

Even though the premise of the last chapter was that you don't
have to know everything to defend your faith, this chapter calls
for us to be as prepared as possible. As we develop a strategy to
defend and share our faith, I can't overemphasize that you must
be ready to do so. This may sound a bit patronizing, as if we don't
already know that we must be prepared. Even so, it is a point that
must be made. How often do we begin our day with the mind-set
to glorify God by leading others to Him? Most of my days begin
with trying to figure out just how long I can stay in bed and still
get to work on time. And honestly, it doesn't get much better as
the day goes on. My attention doesn't shift away from selfish pur-
suits very easily. Yet, despite these egocentric tendencies, we must

be prepared to defend our faith because people will ask about the hope within us.

A City on a Hill

If you live differently than others, people will ask why. We are curious creatures, and when we discover something different, we typically react in one of two ways. Either we want to copy it or we want to destroy it because it seems to threaten our way of life. One thing we will not do is ignore something new and strange.

As you live your life according to Christian values, people will notice that you are different, and they will want to know why. Authentic Christians are lights in a dark world. Their holy lifestyles are beacons of hope. Like a city on a hill, they are impossible to miss. People notice hopeful people in a world of despair, and if you are living a God-honoring life marked by hope in Jesus, you should expect people to ask questions.

It can be strangely comforting to know that others will question your faith. I know to some the very idea is terrifying, but understanding what we are talking about here—relational apologetics—can revolutionize your views about sharing your faith. The idea of evangelism has been tainted by door-to-door salesmen evangelists, angry men on street corners holding offensive signs about God's judgment, and missionaries in white dress shirts riding bicycles on crowded streets. We imagine that to preach the gospel we must become people we do not want to be and go places we do not want to go.

But when your lifestyle is holy, evangelism is much less awkward. It starts happening naturally as opportunities come to you. It turns into respectful conversations at your neighbor's house rather than a stranger's. It becomes the gentle answering of your colleague's questions that arise because of some crisis in the news. It becomes the inevitable talks about a creator that happen while mountain biking with friends. Because people see in your actions the light of your hope, they will ask about your God in the most natural ways. All you need to do is be prepared for the questions.[1]

Preparation for the Defense of Our Faith

Being prepared to answer questions about your faith involves two things: (1) a proper heart attitude that guides and directs your words and actions; and (2) knowledge that will help you answer questions and explain why you have hope in Jesus. Often we think that defending our faith is just about knowing what to say. Knowledge is important but it can be dangerous if it is not accompanied by a pure heart. Knowledge often leads to arrogance, and arrogance is an enemy of the gospel. When it comes to defending your faith, you must first prepare your heart so that you will use your knowledge in loving ways.

A Prepared Heart

A prepared heart believes that Jesus is the uniquely marvelous King of all things—the holy and powerful God, worthy of love and allegiance. It recognizes that Jesus is not just something added to one's life. It understands that He is not some cosmic magician who caters to our whims and flighty desires. Rather, a prepared heart believes that Jesus is the supremely good Ruler of the universe, the Lord to whom it should surrender.

Many of us would agree with these truths about Jesus. We proclaim them in our songs and our prayers. We affirm them in our church creeds. But believing them in our hearts is quite another matter. Our hearts often deceive us; they make us believe things that are not real. Perhaps the greatest struggle of life is convincing our heart that it should desire and serve Jesus above all things. You know this struggle. You can relate with the great hymnist Robert Robinson who pleaded:

---

1. I am not suggesting that evangelism is never hard or uncomfortable. Sometimes natural ways are hostile ways; a person whose mother just passed away will bring you angry, difficult questions. But when you are pursuing holiness and readiness, opportunities to share the gospel abound.

> Prone to wander, Lord, I feel it,
> Prone to leave the God I love;
> Here's my heart, O take and seal it,
> Seal it for Thy courts above.[2]

Wandering from Jesus is common to us all. So often we succumb to the temptation of believing that there are things better than Jesus, and we run to them. We stray from the God we love, and we begin to regard other things as Lord. However, we must fight daily to keep Jesus first. Every day we each must convince our heart of the truth that there is nothing as good as Jesus, nothing to be desired as much as Jesus, and nothing to be loved more than Jesus. Jesus is worthy to be our Lord, to be the unrivaled first in our lives.

As you daily seek to regard Jesus as holy and Lord, your heart will develop the proper attitude to defend your faith. You will not defend your faith to sound smart, win arguments, or hear yourself talk. Your defense will not be done out of obligation or arrogance. Rather, it will flow out of your love for God and your love for others. It will be an extension of your love for the great King and your sole desire to be His ambassador.

A Prepared Mind

The right heart attitude is essential to defend your faith, but you must also have a mind and a mouth that are prepared to explain the reasons for your hope. We want to be able to say something more than "Well, I just have faith" to the skeptic who asks why we believe in God. Saying "the reason I believe in God is because I have faith" is akin to saying, "I hope in God because I hope in God and I hope I'm not wrong." This is not a good enough answer.

The person who asks why you have hope in Jesus wants to know how you *know* that Christianity is true. Among all the options

---

2. Robert Robinson, "Come, Thou Fount of Every Blessing," 1757. Public domain.

available when it comes to religion, why do you choose Jesus? When this question comes, you must be able to offer something more substantial than your subjective feelings. You need to provide reasons for what you believe (offensive apologetics) and answers for skeptical accusations (defensive apologetics). The final portion of this book is designed to help you do these things, but at this point, you simply need to know your reasons for believing in Jesus.

Most Christians never think about why they believe; they just believe. But if you are going to be ready to say why you believe in something, you must think about it before someone asks. And so, I ask you now: Why do you place your hope in Jesus? If you have not thought much about this, I encourage you to stop reading and start thinking about it now. Seriously, right now. Stop and think. Write down all the reasons for your faith in Jesus. If, at the end of your thinking, you have come up with no good reason, hopefully the remainder of this book can provide you with good reasons to have hope in Him.[3]

We cannot be like an ostrich and stick our head in the sand when it comes to the reasons for our hope. We must face the difficult questions about our faith. Facing these questions is something I do on my own, and it has prepared me to answer many skeptics' questions. It has even caused my wife to call me smart, which is a nice bonus; whereas many people think, *I should have said . . .* , my wife tells me I always say those "things" in the conversation. I appreciate her compliment, but if I say the "right things," it's not because I'm particularly smart. I certainly have had many moments when I wished I

---

3. I am not advocating relativistic thinking here. Nor am I defending the "no one can argue with your personal testimony" camp. But there is no magic formula to evangelism. You cannot fully know another person's past. You have no access to their heart and the present work of God in their life. You have no idea what might connect with them. What compelled you to trust in Christ might be what compels another. So you do have the freedom to give personal, subjective reasons for believing in Christ. It cannot be all that is in your toolbox, but you are allowed to use it.

would have said something more or something else. And when I have
no answer to something, it bugs me to no end and I think about it
for a long time. Sometimes I write down the responses I should have
said just to organize my thoughts. Hopefully then, the next time I am
asked the same question, I have a good response.

My "smartness" is just my obsession to think about things longer
than most people. Einstein did this.[4] I've been told he said, "It's not
that I'm so smart, it's just that I stay with problems longer." Christians
who want to explain their hope in Jesus must do this. Stick with the
problems that skeptics have about God long enough to form good answers. Eliminate as many "I should have said" statements as possible.

The Ready Apologist

Someday you will be asked to explain why you have hope in Jesus.
Prepare your heart and prepare your mind. It is loving to do this.
Jesus tells us to love our neighbor as ourselves, and perhaps the great-
est way to love our neighbor is to be able to introduce them to Jesus.

I know this may seem overwhelming, like a mountain of knowledge and holiness to climb. But remember that our God is great and
He will supply you with all that you need. All we need to do is take
the first step in obedience. With that in mind, here are five practical
ways to start.

1. Pray.

Pray each day that God will soften your heart to love others. Pray
that He will open your eyes to opportunities to share the gospel. Pray
that He will help you love Him more than your own safety and respect. Pray that He will increase your knowledge. Pray that He will
go before you into all the situations you will experience and fight the
battles that you could never win on your own. Do not underestimate
the power of your God. Ask Him for help.

---

4. Yes, you can mock me because I indirectly compared myself to Einstein.

2. *Recognize your own sin.*

Being aware of your own sin will help you have compassion for those who do not know Christ. Remembering that Christ has forgiven you creates in you a humble heart, one that desires others to be forgiven just as you have been. He who has been forgiven much, loves much (Luke 7:47). By contrast, when you do not focus on God's grace in your life, you easily become judgmental.

3. *Read your Bible.*

It is amazing how many Christians do not know their Bible. If you don't know the Bible, chances are you do not know why you have hope; worse, you may have reasons that are unbiblical or of no use.[5] Besides, reading your Bible is one way for you to get to know better the God whom you are defending. It is kind of backward to help another person know God when you have no desire to know Him yourself. So start reading your Bible.

4. *Read books like this.*

This book is just a starting place in gaining knowledge; it is not the final destination. There are so many books that can help you know how to answer those who have questions. It is an act of love on your part to study and have as many good answers as possible. At the end of this book I have included a detailed list and summary of many good books that can help you answer skeptics' objections.

5. *Talk with Christians you respect.*

Sometimes the only way to understand something is to talk about

---

5. Current statistics indicate that less than 20 percent of Christians have a biblical worldview. For example, see "Barna Survey Examines Changes in Worldview Among Christians Over the Past Thirteen Years." Barna Group. Last modified March 6, 2009. https://www.barna.org/barna-update/21-transformation/252 -barna-survey-examines-changes-in-worldview-among-christians-over-the- past-13-years#.VPYjDkvkahM

it with others and work through the things that you don't quite understand. Often we don't grasp ideas until we hear them said aloud and discussed. Talking with other Christians is also an excellent way to find answers for your own questions. You gain wisdom and experience from men and women of God who have experienced situations similar to the ones you will experience. Do not attempt to fight the Christian fight alone.

Chapter Four

Gentleness and Respect

But in your hearts honor Christ the Lord as holy,
always being prepared to make a defense to anyone
who asks you for a reason for the hope that is in you;
yet do it with gentleness and respect.
—1 PETER 3:15

Removing Yourself as a Distraction

Defending your faith begins with who you are rather than what you know. Our primary responsibility is to allow the gospel to be seen; the power to save someone rests in the gospel and not in us or in our arguments. However, our lives often hide the goodness of the gospel. Our sinful, hypocritical lifestyles distract from the saving message of the cross. We must remove ourselves as a distraction.

Chapter 1 was about removing the distraction of hypocrisy. This chapter is similar in that it focuses on removing another distraction: the way you treat people. Christians often treat people badly, especially when witnessing. We can be rude, arrogant know-it-alls, who get easily frustrated and speak in condemning ways. Contrary to our intentions, we turn people away from Jesus because of how we act.

This tendency may seem like hypocrisy to you, and on one level you would be right. It is highly hypocritical to thank God for the mercy He has shown you but then refuse to extend mercy to others. It is hypocritical to have received God's love and patience and kindness and not give them to others. Even when people don't deserve respect because of how they are acting, the gospel dictates that we still act in a loving manner. Not giving people what they deserve is at the heart of the Christian message. How often does God not give us what we deserve? We are glad that God's actions are not reactions to our behavior. We are glad that God loved us and died for us while we were still His enemies (Rom. 5:6–11). So when we treat others badly because they "deserve" it, we contradict the message of the gospel.

The Gospel Standard

Being consistent with the gospel means our outward appearance reflects love and compassion, regardless of how we feel inside. While we should always treat people with gentleness and respect, it's especially important when sharing the gospel. But we are only able to do this if we master our feelings instead of being mastered by them.

We live in a day when emotions control people's lives. What we feel, we do. The word "feel" even replaces the word "think" in many comments about things we believe: "I feel like he would be a good person for the job." "I feel like she was trying to say this." "I feel like we should turn left." I feel like we feel things more than we think things these days! But we must counter our culture and master our feelings for the sake of the gospel. Emotions belong in the passenger's seat, not behind the steering wheel.

What you feel about a person should have little bearing on how you treat them. And it's not hypocritical to treat someone differently than how you feel. When people drive you crazy, you are not a hypocrite when you don't punch them in the mouth. When you meet people who hold ridiculous views, you are not a hypocrite when you don't call them stupid. Just because something is true, you don't have free rein to say it. It is okay—even advisable, sometimes—not to tell someone what you are thinking.

Withholding truth is not lying. Truth is powerful and must be used wisely. You must always consider what the person will do with the truth you give them. Are they ready for it? Will they misunderstand it and abuse it because of a presupposition that must be addressed first? Why are you giving it to them? Is it because it is the right thing to say or because you know it will hurt them, make you look good, or merely allow you to win the argument? When defending your faith, responding to the questioner is more important than responding to the question.

Being gentle and respectful means giving people the truth they need to hear, not merely the truth you want them to hear. Often people say, "Well, it's the truth!" as a way to justify the pain or confusion their words caused. As with all things, we must be good stewards of truth. Knowing when to give it is just as important as having the boldness to do so.

Getting Out of the Gospel's Way

Have you ever had a conversation with a disrespectful person, a loud, arrogant know-it-all? How did you feel? How much stock did you put in his words? You probably felt small, and at some point you probably quit listening. His tone and attitude canceled out anything good he might have had to say. Christians must not be this way.

When people hate us, let it not be because we were arrogant or treated them badly. I say, "*when* people hate us," because even gentleness and respect do not guarantee a favorable response. We cannot eliminate all persecution. Still, even though gentleness and respect can't guarantee a positive response to the gospel, at least they don't prohibit one. And that alone is our responsibility in evangelism. We remove obstacles to the gospel, whether ourselves or some bad

philosophy. Then, we speak the gospel and trust the Holy Spirit to
guide minds and convict hearts.

Some Practical Advice

I know it can be difficult not to get angry when sharing your faith.
Others are rude, conversations get frustrating, and the fear of rejection raises our guard. A few tips have helped me stay calm and focused in the midst of emotional situations. I will share three of them
with you; I hope they help.

1. Knowledge is a weapon.

I have found that knowledge helps me stay calm. Much of our anger stems from the frustration of not knowing what to say or the
inability to say what we mean. I remember the freedom I found from
my emotions in college after reading several books about defending my faith. Just having this knowledge kept me from getting angry in conversations because I was less frustrated about what to say.
Knowledge is a weapon, and when we are armed we are less anxious.
Like water for fire, knowledge puts out the flames of anger fueled by
frustration.

2. Conversations can end.

I have learned that the present conversation is not necessarily the
most important one. You can end a talk with a skeptic before they
get saved. Often we feel the burden of trying to save someone in our
first conversation. Though a sense of urgency in evangelism is right,
it is also right to understand that many people will not respond to the
gospel the first time they hear it.

We are often told that our one conversation might be the only
time someone ever hears the gospel. That may be true, but when that
burden becomes a pressure, it surfaces in frustration and anger and
works against the gospel. More often than not, skeptics need to hear
the gospel more than once before they respond. So don't be angry and

surprised when they don't immediately agree with you. Expect them to disagree. Understand that their disagreement is probably not a result of your inability to communicate well. The skeptic's problem is not primarily with you; it is with your God. You are an ambassador. Their rejection of God is not about you, so don't take it personally.

3. Skeptics are people too.

I have learned that many people of differing beliefs are good people and can be good friends. Don't misunderstand what I mean by "good" people. (I can hear the protests of preachers quoting Psalm 14.) What I mean is that we often view people who don't believe in God as our enemies. Too many of us, friendship with a non-Christian seems like a sin.

But friendship with people who don't believe in God is a good thing as long as you are the influencer. You will have to determine the depth of your friendship through prayer and counsel, because the more you hang around someone, the more you act and think like them. However, Jesus Himself was the friend of sinners. You can and should view non-Christians as people you can befriend. Often this friendship is what it will take for them to see the truth of the gospel.

A Success Story

I have not always been good at what we are talking about here. I am sarcastic and opinionated. I naturally think I am right and you are wrong. I am competitive and I can be hotheaded. I am an awful person. But I have learned the value of staying calm and treating people with respect in conversations. It is something that I work on, and I'd like to end this chapter with one of my success stories. (I am apparently an old man now because I love to tell stories. It's probably about time I get a good rocking chair and a pipe, but I'll proceed without them.)

Working with teenagers for nearly twenty years has given me a treasure of stories. Several years ago I befriended a skeptical couple, a boy and a girl who were dating and were both skeptical about God and the Christian message. These two dressed differently, didn't go to church, liked vampires, were smart, and thought Christianity was stupid. "Stupid" may be too strong a word, but they definitely didn't think the Christian message held up to reason. There were other Christians in their lives, but not many of them treated this pair very well.

I talked a great deal with them about my faith in Jesus. I also asked them many questions about what they believed. I took an interest in what they liked. I learned about *Doctor Who* and I was introduced to dubstep. I asked them to play their music for me, and we would talk about the movies they liked. I liked them. I truly liked them. I considered them my friends. I also disagreed with what they believed and made it my job to help them see the folly of their beliefs. I did this mainly by asking questions. I asked how they explained the creation of the universe. I questioned why they thought morals existed. I asked for one thing about Christianity that made them think it might be true.[1] I also asked for their biggest reason for rejecting Christianity. Guess what they said. More than anything else, they said, it was the hypocrisy of Christians.[2]

Now, these two were smart. They had intellectual objections to the Christian faith. Yet their biggest problem with Christianity was the people. What makes this so bothersome is that they had been involved in youth groups and other Christian organizations for most of their lives. It appears that a lifetime of interaction with Christ's followers was more powerful than anything else to convince them that God didn't exist.

I felt sorry for them, and I told them so. I told them that the hypocrisy in Christians is a fair reason to have an issue with their message.

---

1. This answer was interesting. They said it was the fact that so many people believe it to be true.
2. As a side note: it is really interesting that their biggest objection to Christianity and their biggest reason why it may be true were the same—Christians.

Then I asked if it was enough evidence for them to reject God, or if it would be a mistake to write God off because some of His followers were jerks. They conceded that "bad" Christians were enough to make them think the message was false but not enough to prove God didn't exist. Then they said something I didn't expect. They thanked me for being the only Christian that had ever treated them with respect. They told me that the way I treated them made them want to talk with me. They appreciated that I recognized their intelligence, and I didn't make them look stupid. They told me that my respect for them caused them to consider my message. Now, I have been trained in apologetics. I believe I have good arguments. But it was my gentleness and respect and not my words that caused them to consider Christianity.

The Loving Apologist

I learned much from this couple. I learned that words mean nothing if I do not love people and treat them with respect. Obviously, words have their place. If you don't think so, go ask a mime for directions. Actions don't speak, and the gospel must be spoken for it to be heard and believed. Love without direction is futile, but so is direction without love. Direction without love only perpetuates rebellion. Therefore, we must be balanced people who love with our actions *and* love with our words. One without the other just will not do.

Part Two

What You Do

Chapter Five

Listen

I like to listen. I have learned a great deal from
listening carefully. Most people never listen.
—ERNEST HEMINGWAY

The Art of Listening

Most of what we have discussed so far has pertained to who you are. This is because a healthy apologetic for Christianity rests on a solid foundation in your life. You must be committed to Christ if you are to lead others to Him. We don't want to be hypocrites, and furthermore, only as holy people will we have the pure heart and renewed mind essential in evangelism. But now we're shifting away from who you are and considering some practical relational skills and conversational strategies. We will begin with the most important skill: the ability to listen.

Listening is a hard skill to develop. Not many people are good at it. Most people like to talk more than listen because it gives them the opportunity to sound smart, win arguments, convince people they're right, and be the center of attention. While I have just painted us—perhaps a bit harshly—as self-absorbed egomaniacs, this is often why we talk.

Whether this self-centeredness is true of you or not, my point is that conversations are typically one-sided affairs, where people tolerate the noise from other people's mouths only because it gives them the chance to say something themselves. In a fast-paced world where we fear being left behind, we talk to be noticed, and listening becomes a secondary concern.

The Love of Listening

I challenge you to enter conversations with the mind-set of listening instead of talking. This happens only after we have resolved in our hearts to love others the way Christ loved us. And how did Christ love us? He gave His life for us. He did not look to gain anything from us. Rather, He gave Himself fully. This is how we should engage the skeptic in conversations—with the mind-set of serving. And we cannot serve others until we know what they need, and we only know what they need by listening.

Listening shows that we care, that we aren't simply out to win. So often conversations about faith quickly turn into a competition to outsmart the other person. You know. You have been there. You have experienced what it is like to be sucked into a heated debate about God or religion. You know what it is like to feel your blood boil. And you know how easily your good intention to witness gets lost in emotions and competition when someone belittles your beliefs.

The Power of Listening

Listening helps you avoid confrontational situations because it helps both you and the conversation remain calm. Conversation can be like a fire, and words are its fuel. Quite practically, the fewer words you use in a conversation the less kindling there is for fire. The more you let someone else talk, the more fuel they use up, and the quicker their fire dies.

I have been in situations where someone starts speaking, passionately speaking,[1] and all I do is let them talk. I don't interrupt. I don't ask questions. I don't offer a rebuttal. I just let them finish talking. Often what happens is their fire burns out. They get out what they were thinking and feeling, and without any interruption or inflammatory words on my part, they calm down, and then we can talk some more.

Listening also helps you remain calm because it often produces compassion. I am not exactly sure why this is, but when I practice the art of listening and don't just focus on what I am going to say next, I find that I start to have compassion for the other person.

Most people are not villains or bad friend material. Yet, when we only focus on what people say that we disagree with, and then start plotting how to attack them with our words when they shut up, in our minds they become an enemy. People who disagree do not have to be opponents. Listening helps us see the individual behind the belief.

When you listen, and listen well, you are listening not only to people's words but also to their tone and the feelings they convey. You can see that they are hurting or that they feel alone. You can sense the bitterness from something in their past. You can see that they are just like you. When you listen well, you see a person and not just an opposing position.

The Purpose of Listening

Listening is also important because you need to understand the position of the person with whom you are speaking. I am sure this is obvious to you. Yet I cannot tell you how many times I have overheard people arguing about something that was never said. Communication can be quite tricky. It's hard sometimes to say what you mean. It's even harder to communicate when the other person isn't listening and, instead, is assuming.

Most people assume they know what you are going to say, and they

---

1. This is my nice way of saying they are angry and getting emotional.

assume they know what you mean. They do this because they read into comments more than they listen to them. Often we put people and their beliefs in categories without really listening to them. Then we respond to the position or belief we think they have instead of trying to find out exactly what they believe and why.

Recently, two friends of mine, Bob and Butch, were discussing the existence of hell. At one point, Butch commented that Jesus' teachings on hell were ambiguous. Butch's words, unbeknownst to him, were virtually identical to those in a popular new book that rejects the existence of hell, a position Butch doesn't hold.

Butch and the book may both share the belief that Jesus was ambiguous about hell, but Butch didn't think this was proof that hell didn't exist. But guess what Bob did. He immediately assumed that Butch agreed with the position of the book—that is, that hell doesn't exist. He read the beliefs of others into Butch's comments and stopped listening. Bob assumed he knew what Butch was saying, and instead of listening further, he began to argue over a position that Butch didn't even hold.

We must avoid this type of situation. We must control our emotions and our tongues. We must listen fully, not just respond when we hear something we don't like or agree with. Many things work against us when we defend our faith. We do not need misunderstanding to be one of them.

The Listening Apologist

If you want to defend your faith well, become a good listener. Be patient and hear what others are saying so that you can respond appropriately. Do not dominate conversations. This is not easy. It takes practice. But you need to do it. Let me offer four practical ways to improve your listening.

1. Focus on their words and not your response.

Nearly everyone devises clever retorts or responses while the other person is talking, and it is no different in conversations of faith. This isn't actually a conversation. It's two people lecturing an audience that isn't paying attention, and it's not effective.

You need to practice not thinking about your response when someone else is talking. This is hard. It is a discipline that you can learn, though. When you notice you're forming a response before they are done speaking, stop and refocus. Witnessing to skeptics is usually a marathon. You must pace yourself. Don't try to sprint to the end. Don't worry about jumping in and rebutting everything they say as soon as they say it. Rather, slow down, trust in the power of the Holy Spirit to remind you of the truth, and do not worry about winning.

2. Ask questions.

This is actually what the next chapter is about, but I'll give you a bit of it here. If the person you are talking with is long-winded and hard to follow, ask them to restate their belief or position slowly and concisely. Remember, it is vital that you understand what they believe before you respond, so ask a question if you didn't catch it the first time.

You can do this by asking them to summarize what they just said. What I find effective is to summarize what I think they just said and say it back to them. Typically when someone has finished talking I will say something like, "So let me make sure I understood you. You believe that . . ." This is effective because it ensures that I understand them. I often find that when I do this people see how their position is flawed, which is just a bonus.

3. Write down their points.

Stopping conversations to jot down others' points of contention is so simple and practical and will revolutionize your apologetic efforts. This practice is valuable in several ways. It keeps conversations calm and focused. It gives you time to think. It ensures that you heard correctly. It gives you their points to study later without relying on your memory. And it lets others see their position laid out neatly for perhaps the first time.

You will find many people have not thought through their beliefs; it isn't only Christians who have not contemplated their religion. The goal of listening is hearing, and by hearing, I mean comprehending. Seeing beliefs ordered on paper allows everyone to clearly understand the position. Many times, this process does the work for the apologist by showing skeptics the inconsistency or inherent contradictions in their beliefs.

4. Pray.

One of the things I do when talking with a skeptic is to pray short prayers throughout the conversation. In just a couple of words I ask God for wisdom, control of my emotions, and the ability to hear what the other person is saying. I also ask God to help me understand why they think like they do. It is good to ask God to give you eyes that can see past arguments into motives. Clever words are often a smoke screen for a deeper issue. Arguments that appear logical may be covering some emotional or volitional problem.[2] People's default position is to believe in God (Rom. 1:19–32). In their attempt to hide from Him, people devise wise-sounding arguments to convince themselves that they are right in their rebellion. Ask God for wisdom to see why they are rebelling.

Praying throughout the conversation is an act of faith whereby you understand that it is the Lord who draws people to Himself, and you are but a tool in the process. It will keep you humble and calm. It will keep you focused on the well-being of the other person and keep

---

2. Volition pertains to the will. Often rebellion against God manifests itself in intellectual ways. Some people know that God exists, yet they do not want to bow to Him, and so they create intellectual reasons why they shouldn't. People can know truth but suppress it and come up with reasons to justify their rebellion.

you from becoming consumed with winning. All of this helps you listen. And beyond the benefit of listening, it keeps you relying on the Lord and not your wisdom, and this is right where you want to be in dealing with a skeptic. So pray, pray, pray.

Chapter Six

Ask Questions

The important thing is to never stop asking questions.
Curiosity has its own reason for existing.
—ALBERT EINSTEIN

A Good Friend and a Good Question

If I could be anyone other than myself, there are a few people that I wouldn't mind being. One of them is my friend Cameron Ford. One particular incident from our high school days shows the kind of guy he is. On this occasion, we went to see a movie with another friend. The show times were visible from our car, and as we sat in the car thinking about how to waste eight bucks on some mindless nonsense, a pair of intoxicated young lads came our way. They apparently thought we were looking at them, and the taller one said, "You got a problem? Whatcha lookin' at?"

Now, I confess that I am prone to be a sarcastic jerk and often cannot keep my mouth shut, especially when my manhood is being called into question. So, instead of calmly telling the nice young man that I wasn't looking at him, but was simply trying to see what movies were playing, I responded to the irate ruffian, now in my face, by saying, "Problem? You're in my face. What do you want . . . a kiss?" This did not help our situation. He immediately stepped back and slurred, "Ahh nah, this dude's a gay! I'm gonna punch this guy in the face!"

At this point, I realized my stupidity and braced myself for a punch to the face. I don't know why we didn't think to drive away or roll up the window—but boys will be boys (which means stupid). I raised my arm to block the blow when Cameron said from the back seat, "Dude, why are you so angry?"

It was as if Cameron had cast a spell on the guy about to punch me. He froze and simply said, "Uh . . . I don't know." His rage melted away instantly because of a simple question. The happy ending is that I didn't get punched in the face, Cameron offered the gospel, and the guy apologized to us—all because Cameron asked a question.

The Power of a Question

A great companion to the skill of listening is the ability to ask a good question. Questions are powerful. They make us stop and think. We often don't know why we do what we do or think what we think. Questions make us consider our beliefs and actions. This is good. Many beliefs have no good reason to exist, but they have become part of our lives over many unthinking years.

God asks questions. It is one of the first things we see Him doing in the Bible. When Adam and Eve hid because they had sinned, God asked, "Where are you?" The ensuing conversation contained two more questions: "Who told you that you were naked?" and "What have you done?" Then in the very next chapter of Genesis, God asks more questions. This time He asks Cain, "Why are you so angry?" and then, after Cain had killed Abel, "What have you done?"[1]

Now I ask you a question: why does an all-knowing God ask questions? Surely He knew what Adam, Eve, and Cain had done better

---

1. See Genesis 3–4.

than they did. So why did God ask? Did He need help figuring out what had just happened and what He should do next? The answer is obviously no, and so it must be that the questions were not for God's benefit but man's.

The questions that God asks are intended to help us explain our own actions, look inward at our motives, and see our own folly. That is one reason Jesus asked so many questions. Notice in the Gospels how many questions He asked and how many were left unanswered. Jesus often left people confused. Why would He do this? The reason is that questions make people think, while statements make them defend. Jesus' questions prompted people to examine their beliefs and assumptions.

Beliefs are personal. They become part of us, part of our identities even. Ever notice how no one says your belief is wrong? Instead, they say *you* are wrong. It is hard not to feel personally attacked in this situation. And therein is the value of questions. They facilitate the examination of beliefs while minimizing the possibility that a person will feel attacked. And when someone feels safe, they can think.

Avoiding the War of Words

A conversation about faith can easily turn into a war of words. What may have begun as a loving attempt to show someone the truth of the gospel can quickly become a battle of wills and emotions. Defenses are raised and weapons are sharpened.

Asking questions is a way to bypass the defenses that easily arise in conversations of faith. First, questions often don't seem like an attack. This is not always true, though, since body language and tone can make even a phrase like "you look nice" an insult. But for the most part, sincere questions carefully asked can get past common defenses in conversations about faith and actually cause the attack on a person's beliefs to come from within. As another good friend of mine says, "A question is a powerful seed to plant. Nobody wants to be coerced into accepting something to which they are strongly opposed, and asking a simple question rather than telling someone what they should think can provide an effective way through that barrier."[2]

Second, questions move the burden of proof from you to them. Often we feel the weight of needing to have all the answers to any question or accusation that can challenge our beliefs. However, asking questions turns the tables, and instead of using your knowledge to prove something about God, you let the other person probe their knowledge (or lack thereof) about God. Often your question exposes a flaw in their thinking. When it comes to sharing our faith, especially with skeptics, asking questions can be more effective than all the right and irrefutable arguments we can muster.

Say a friend mocks the idea of God always existing. He might say, "Who created God?" You respond, "Well, no one made God." At this point your hands are sweating because you know you are cornered. I mean, how do you prove that no one created God, and what sense does that make anyway? How can something have always existed? You know your friend is thinking this too.

But instead of feeling cornered and just ending the conversation at your friend's next question by saying, "Well, you just have to have faith," ask this question: "If God did not exist to create, where do you think life came from?" The reason you ask this question is because the origin of life is a problem that skeptics also have to answer.

Most skeptics believe their view of the origin of life is rational, unlike the "uneducated theists." If you believe in an uncreated, eternal God, you are foolish. But follow this logic: for the skeptic, life has either evolved from nothing or from preexisting matter. These are their only two choices. The first option makes no sense. How can something come into existence uncaused and out of nothing? Something would first have to exist to bring itself into existence, which is a contradiction and makes no sense.

---

2. Josiah David Haner, "The Art of Knowledge Repression," May 15, 2014, Josiah David blog, http://josiahdavidmusic.com/2014/05/15/knowledgerepression/.

Therefore, for the skeptic, the only logical explanation is that there was some preexisting matter that evolved into everything we know as life. You see the problem, right? The only reasonable position for the skeptic to take is that there was something that has always existed and had no maker, which is exactly what Christians believe.

A simple question can take a tense situation and seemingly irreconcilable positions and create common ground between the skeptic and the believer. There is unity because not all things are fully explainable. We deal in degrees of certainty. The idea of an eternal something is not a truth that can be fully mined and understood. It is not in the two-plus-two family.

The skeptic and the believer stand on very common ground regarding their cosmological beliefs. Neither can claim to have full certainty of their position. And truth be told, there is not much in life that can be known perfectly. For example, is it possible to have complete certainty that the water in your glass will not poison you? Even if you had the means to test it, could the test be wrong? Could you misread the results? Could there be something in your glass that your test cannot discover? Is the appropriate conclusion never to drink water again because you can't be perfectly certain that it is safe?

Despite the claims of the intellectual elite, you need not have total certainty to be justified in believing something. This is not practical, and nobody operates this way. Asking questions can create a level playing field because everyone holds beliefs for which there is not total certainty. There is nothing wrong with this. And, once everyone realizes this, you have a starting point from which you can move on to examine evidence and see whose belief is more justified.

The Questioning Apologist

Asking questions is a valuable tactic to use in defending your faith. Don't forget that other people are also responsible to explain why their way of thinking is better than yours. You do not have to be a punching bag for skeptics who get to throw blow after blow and never defend their own beliefs.

It is okay to lovingly press skeptics for answers on things like why they think God doesn't exist, where life came from, why truth is relative, and so on. When you do, make sure to listen intently so that you can ask more specific questions. Most likely, if you are paying attention, both you and your friend will see some problem with their explanation, and the skeptic may come to realize that his position is not as foolproof as he thought.

I probably ask more questions than I make statements. This has been such a valuable tactic to me.[3] It keeps the pressure off. It allows me to learn a lot about what the other person believes. It helps me stay calm. It creates an actual conversation and not a lecture. And it allows me to gain the respect of the other person. I can't express enough the value of earning respect through genuinely listening and caring for people. Asking questions and listening is kind, and your kindness can be a gateway to their repentance.

---

3. For an in-depth treatment of tactics like asking questions see Greg Koukl, *Tactics: A Game Plan for Discussing Your Christian Convictions* (Grand Rapids: Zondervan, 2009).

Chapter Seven

Stay on Topic

If a situation requires undivided attention, it will occur simultaneously with a compelling distraction.
—HUTCHINSON'S LAW

The Chase

You must learn to not chase rabbits. Conversations easily wander because people are easily distracted and the mind likes to follow whatever shiny new idea enters its domain. However, to be effective in talking about weighty and potentially confusing subjects like God, you must focus on one topic long enough to say something meaningful.

Conversations meander on their own, but they also are purposely taken off course. In logic, this is called a red herring. The story goes that herring, a fish, gains a reddish color and a very strong smell when it is smoked. Because of this smell, red herrings mask other smells. Criminals and hunters alike could drag a red herring across a trail and create a false trail for dogs to follow. By analogy, the phrase "red herring" is used to describe any false trail. Conversation partners may not distract you with smelly fish, but they will often use random facts and irrelevant stories to divert you from the original topic or question. They create false trails, red herrings, for you to follow.

I was talking with a woman once about the nature of truth, and suddenly she exploded with a story about "crazed" Christians blowing up abortion clinics. Then she explained how judgmental and "mental" Christians were. In her mind, there may have been a connection between the existence of truth and Christians blowing up abortion clinics, but if there was, it never came out. This was mainly because I didn't follow the false trail.

When you start to notice people changing topic, bring them back to the original issue. Don't chase every topic that appears in front of you. Stay focused and lead the way back to your original conversation. You can do this simply by saying something like, "I agree that Christians, or anyone for that matter, shouldn't blow up abortion clinics, but let's keep talking about truth." A simple redirect usually works.

Redirecting is a valuable skill. You cannot let others frame discussions for you by bringing unrelated topics into the conversation. Whether intentionally or not, people will create your position for you, a position that likely doesn't even exist. In logic this is known as a straw man fallacy. They set up something that looks real, a straw man, but is easily knocked down. Redirecting allows you to present your real position without the distortion that comes from the intrusion of unrelated topics.

The Switch

There are several reasons why people switch topics. One is that they genuinely think two topics are related. The woman from my example before may have sincerely thought there was a connection between the existence of truth and Christians blowing up abortion clinics. She may have thought that people do extreme things because they are convinced their position is the right one. In our larger conversation, she did say that all truth does is divide people. She added that we should be tolerant of other people's views and not blow things up when we disagree.

I agree with most of what she said. I generally agree that blowing things up is not the answer.[1] But what Christians or anyone else blow up has nothing to do with whether truth is relative or absolute. The existence of truth and people's response to what they believe to be true are separate issues. In our conversation about truth, the woman not only introduced a different topic, she introduced a highly emotional topic. And once that happens, you might as well resign to talk another day. You have lost the battle simply because you started fighting a new one.

A second reason people switch topics is because they know they have been defeated. When faced with a question they cannot answer, people often either make something up or change the subject. We are proud and for many of us admitting defeat is not an option, so we change the subject. A really crafty person can change the subject without the other person knowing.

The abortion debate is a great example of topic switching. The majority of abortion advocates cite a woman's right to choose as the reason that abortion should remain legal. The two sides are pitted against each other as pro-life and pro-*choice*. The pro-choice position is characterized by the belief that a woman has the right to do with her body what she thinks best. But the belief in this right is a separate topic from abortion. Or, at most, it is a secondary topic within the abortion discussion.

The abortion argument is about one thing: whether or not a fetus is a person. This really is the only relevant question. No one would argue that a woman has the right to choose to kill a child. Either a fetus is just matter like a tumor, or it is a person who lives in a womb. If it is matter like a tumor, then doctors and families should have the right

---

1. Unless you are on *MythBusters*, where apparently the answer to everything is to blow something up.

to determine what to do with it. If it is a person who lives in a womb, then it has rights, namely, the right to life. This is what the abortion debate is about. A woman's right to choose is only relevant once the main issue has been settled: is a fetus a person or not?

Do you see how the "right to choose" is merely a crafty way to change the subject? Abortion advocates must defend that a fetus is not a person. However, most of them cannot. This is partly because many have only assumptions about their position and they repeat sound bites when pressed for answers. But even those who have thought about their position still find it difficult to defend that a fetus is not a person. There is no consensus in the medical field or scientific community on when "life" begins, when "the matter" becomes a person.[2] Furthermore, the philosophical reasons usually given to disqualify a fetus from personhood are arbitrary and, in most cases, would eliminate toddlers as well.[3]

Since the average person is not equipped to discuss abortion in terms of personhood, the topic changes. It moves from the status of a fetus to the rights of a woman. It assumes that the real issue of whether a fetus is a person has been settled, and then it moves to a different topic: the woman's right to choose. This is subtle, it is crafty, and it has nothing to do with the original argument.

The Focused Apologist

Don't be overwhelmed. And please don't think you'll never be able to spot things like this. You will. You'll learn to do this as you learn how

---

2. This is primarily because the question of life and personhood is a philosophical discussion, not a scientific or medical one. See *Defending Life: A Moral and Legal Case Against Abortion Choice* by Francis J. Beckwith (New York: Cambridge University Press, 2007) for a detailed analysis of this topic.

3. These reasons include such characteristics as size, level of development, environment, and degree of dependency. This would also exclude certain adults from personhood status. For a detailed analysis of this topic, see Scott Klusendorf, *The Case for Life: Equipping Christians to Engage the Culture* (Wheaton, IL: Crossway, 2009).

to listen and ask questions. You really don't need to know a great deal to be able to stay on topic. If you listen to someone and after they make several points, you aren't sure if they are on topic, ask them. Say something like, "Hang on, I think you just said a couple of different things. I understand how the first one relates to our discussion, but could you explain the second one?" Always feel free to respectfully ask how what they have said relates to what you have been talking about. Brilliant, isn't it? I'm sure right now you're asking yourself why you spent money on this book. But good advice is not always complicated advice.

In conversations of faith, people will say *a lot*. Often they throw out every objection they can think of at once. Most people have not organized and categorized their objections against God; they just know they don't believe in Him. So when you start talking about God, be prepared for them to tell you every reason why they don't believe. Even if your conversation begins with, say, the nature of truth, understand that their position on truth likely falls under the same category as God's existence. So at any point they might bring up something other than what they think about truth as they try to justify their rejection of God.

But all you need to do to stay on topic is to listen well, and, again, if at any point you don't understand how what they said relates to what you were originally talking about, ask. Remember this great truth: the one who makes the claim bears the responsibility of supporting it. It isn't only Christians who have to justify their beliefs. You are allowed to ask others to support their statements. Doing this not only helps you stay on topic, but it often shows the other person that they have no good argument about the original topic.

You must anchor your conversations. Do not let them drift wherever they want. Subjects about religion and God are difficult, and you cannot tackle them all at once. You must focus on one subject at a time and, within that subject, one question at a time. You can do this if you listen and ask questions. Then you will see much more fruit from your conversations.

Chapter Eight

Stick with What You Know

The greatest way to live with honor in this world
is to be what we pretend to be.
—SOCRATES

A Recap

Defending Christianity is done properly by someone who wants to glorify God by pursuing holiness and becoming prepared to share their faith with gentleness and respect. I hope you have seen that defending your faith requires you to focus on who you are as much as what you know. I hope you see that there is a right way to go about this, but that it is also not very complicated. Defending your faith is as simple as being a holy person who is willing to listen to others, ask questions, stay on a chosen topic, and explain why you believe in Jesus.

To conclude this section, I want to offer one last bit of practical advice. I began this book making the point that you don't have to know everything. In this chapter, I want to make sure that you stick with what you know. The burden of proof rests on the person who makes the claim. So, practically speaking, the more you say, the more you have to defend.

The "Expert"

When it comes to "proving" that God exists, people will say almost anything. I have heard all kinds of arguments to prove that Christianity is the right religion. In a sincere attempt to defend their faith, normal everyday Christians instantly become experts and statisticians: "Did you know that 72 percent of the ocean floor is filled with fossils that are indigenous to high altitudes which proves the flood?"[1] You must not be one of these "experts."

It's very easy to be sucked into talking like an expert when you really only know a little bit about something. I had a friend who was the king of this. He was a passionate person, and he was not quiet. He liked to share his beliefs. One day a conversation about the flood in Genesis came up. He instantly chimed in, passionately and angrily explaining that there is not enough water on the planet to cover the tops of the mountains. He went on and on about this, throwing out data about the polar ice caps and how fast mountains grow. I asked him how he knew all of this. He said he read it. I asked where. He said he didn't know. I said, "No offense, but you are no geologist and you may be right, but I am not going to take your word on this. I need to see your evidence." He said he didn't know where he'd read it. He still has not shown it to me.

The point is not that he was factually wrong. Some of what he said may be right, for all I know. But he was not an expert in the field he was lecturing about, yet he expected me to listen to him as if he were. Not only may he have been wrong about much of his information, I knew that he is no expert in this field. His arrogance discredited him even before his words had a chance to. People hate this. I hate this.

---

1. This statistic is completely made up.

I don't listen to people who go on and on about a subject in which I know they are not an expert. You don't either, unless you are a fool. So don't be that type of person.

Unfortunately, Christians are guilty of this all of the time. We read some book on logic and think we are professional apologists and debaters. After reading (and by "reading" I mean glancing over a few chapters) about how the universe points to a creator, we start talking like astronomers. We discover that our bodies are evidence of design and we begin giving presentations as biologists. We are like a boy who hit a homerun in a little league game and thinks he is ready for Yankee Stadium.

The problem is not what we know, but how we use it. It is good to read books. It is good to learn how the universe and its design are indications that God exists. But often these bits of knowledge inflate our sense of expertise and cause us to say more than we can defend. We do this because we sincerely believe that God exists and Jesus is His Son, and we want others to believe it too. So in the attempt to persuade, we pull out what we think is impressive information and irrefutable fact and then present it with the confidence and experience of a professional. This approach does not work. The authority and superiority of the Christian worldview does not need you to bolster its case by presenting yourself as something other than you are. What is more likely to happen is that your dishonest representation will undermine your claims.

The Dangers of Being an "Expert"

Christians must only speak about things with the level of experience and expertise they actually have. People are led to Christ every day by those without advanced degrees. Besides, it is dangerous to talk like an expert. When you talk like an expert—but aren't one—you leave the door wide open for mistakes. When you haven't mastered a field of study, you are prone to misunderstand its content. You inevitably will say something wrong about it—misquote statistics, draw wrong conclusions, or just get confused and use information in the wrong context. A little bit of knowledge is a dangerous thing and acting like an expert will eventually make you look like a fool.

But making mistakes is only part of the problem. The more you say in an argument, the more you have to defend. When you make a claim, you are responsible to support what you say. It is your job to be able to prove that it is true. You aren't allowed to throw out statements without the ability to support them. So don't offer information that you don't know much about, because the chances are good you will have to back it up.

For example, let's say you claim that the Bible is historically reliable. You say something like, "The Bible has been proven to be historically reliable, so whatever it says about Jesus must be true." Sounds like a good argument, right? But what happens when your skeptic friend asks how you know this? What do you do when you're asked who proved its historical reliability? What do you say when you're asked which Bible? Some Bibles include the Apocrypha. Are they historically reliable too? What about the contradictions in the Bible? Doesn't one gospel say that there were two angels at Jesus' tomb and another says there was one?

My point is not to scare you into silence, but to show what happens when you make a claim. The more you say, the more you need to defend. So if you are not prepared to enter a discussion about the historical reliability of the Bible, don't throw out random quotes and statistics about it. What you know about the reliability of the Bible may be sufficient for your understanding of it, but teaching it or defending it is a different matter.

The Correct Use of Knowledge

So how do we use the knowledge we have and avoid getting in trouble by acting like an expert? Here is what I suggest. Let's use the previous example. If you can't defend the historical reliability of the

Bible, don't bring it up. If someone asks you about it, that's another matter. And in that case, you have two options.

One option is to say, "I don't know." "I don't know" is a much safer and effective response than saying something that is wrong or can't be supported. Not knowing something shows only that you don't know everything, but being wrong shows that you draw bad conclusions from data. This hurts the gospel because it allows the skeptic to assume that if you're wrong about the Bible's historical reliability, you're likely also wrong about things like the resurrection of Jesus Christ.

Another option, and I think a better one, is to say what you think and then offer to study the topic with the skeptic. In the present scenario, you could say something like, "I believe that the Bible has been proven to be historically reliable. I have read that it was, but I'm no expert. I would love to learn more about it. Would you want to study it with me?"

By asking to study something with your friend, you have accomplished two things. First, you haven't come across like an expert. Instead you appear humble and honest. You have shown that you are committed to finding truth, not just defending a personal belief. It shows that you respect the other person. This is all very good.

Second, if your friend says yes, you have established a relationship that will be ongoing. Many people act like snipers in conversations with skeptics: one shot and they're out. However, we should treat conversations like mountain climbing, a long process that requires careful steps and great preparation. Establishing ongoing relationships with skeptics is very important. Remember that they likely have had years to think about their position and let their heart grow hard toward God. Expect it to take time for them to see Jesus. Then praise the Lord if it happens quickly.

The Reasonable Apologist

Understand that there are no magic words to defend your faith other than the gospel. The gospel has the power to break through anything and save. The power of the Holy Spirit is unparalleled, but your words are not. Don't think that one impressive statistic or fact is going to overpower years of rebellion and skepticism. So don't stretch what you know and make claims you can't back up.

Sticking with what you know is the second best piece of advice I have ever received in terms of defending the faith (learning to ask good questions is probably the first). It shows that you are a reasonable person, one who is not prone to overreacting and making foolish decisions based on wrong information. It makes you credible, forcing the skeptic to wonder if you are right. If you can't be proven wrong, and skeptics are honest, they will reconsider their position.

You may be thinking I am telling you never to be wrong, that you should only talk about the things you know well. You are correct; I am. Strive for perfection. You will, of course, make mistakes and you will end up being wrong sometimes, and that is okay. But prepare meticulously and set your standard high. Guard the presentation of the gospel. Honor truth by putting limits on what you say. Don't let this keep you from speaking, but let it guide what you share.

Don't be surprised by this high standard—as if I would tell you to say whatever you want in a conversation, even if it is wrong, just so you can win the debate. Love people by respecting them. Talk about what you know, humbly admit what you don't, and commit yourself to study more, both alone and with skeptics, whenever you have the chance. I encourage you to know what you know and know it well. Fearlessly proclaim the gospel, and fearlessly be willing to look weak when you reach the limits of your knowledge.

Part Three

What You Know

Chapter Nine

Truth

Half a truth is often a great lie.
—BENJAMIN FRANKLIN

It's All Relative?

My daughter is a relativist. It surfaced at age two. One day my wife and I saw our sweet little devil bite her brother. We pulled her aside and told her that she is not allowed to bite. Here's what happened next:

"K.K., you are not allowed to bite your brother."

"I didn't."

"Yes, you did. We saw you."

"No, I did not bite him!"

"K.K., we saw you. You need to tell the truth."

"I did not bite him and that is my truth!"

Though my daughter flaunts relativistic thinking, she is pretty discriminate in her wielding of "personal truths." When the shoe is on the other foot, she does not afford her brother the luxury of having a personal truth regarding *his* teeth marks on her arm.

You are probably familiar with relativism, the philosophical position that all beliefs are equally valid and are relative to the individual. Relativism basically means that people get to decide for themselves what is true and what isn't. Even if you aren't familiar with the word "relativism," you have most likely met someone or heard of someone who said, "Well, that's just my personal truth! What's true for me doesn't have to be true for you!"

But most of us recognize that no one is consistently a relativist. Everyone has exclaimed at some point, "That's not fair!"—a statement that indicates there is a standard for appropriate behavior. In fact, it is impossible to be a consistent relativist. We all hold certain beliefs that we expect others to follow. For example, none of us think it's okay if someone steals from us, and none of us are likely to say that racism is a valid personal belief. No one lives like a relativist.

Human behavior undermines this philosophy about truth, but so does logic. Consider this claim: "All truth is relative." Is this a relative truth? Or is it a claim that all people should believe? You see the problem. For relativism to have any value, this claim must be true. It must correspond to reality, the way things really are. But can it be absolutely true that truth is relative? That is nonsense. Relativism is a self-defeating proposition.

The Death of Relativism

Relativism came to popularity in Western culture, where the dominant worldview was the Christian worldview. Ideas like sin and repentance were accepted and normal. Biblical precepts gave society its moral boundaries. Those who chose to live outside those boundaries needed to do one of two things: convince people that their actions were not wrong or erase the idea of wrong altogether. Rather than persuade others that their beliefs were right, crafty and deceitful men and women perpetuated the idea that we are all right.

When truth is not on your side or you have no power, you need relativism. When you are not in a position to make people do what you think is right, a clever way to justify your own "personal right" is to propagate the idea that everyone is right. So pop philosophy and its bumper stickers gave us statements like "That's just my personal truth" and "What's true for me doesn't have to be true for you." And the more people heard these things, the more they started thinking in non-absolute terms. Add to that a good dose of skepticism and philosophical rhetoric, and suddenly people thought that even if truth does exist, we have no way to know it. For centuries, this relativistic philosophy eroded the notion of absolute truth from western society and gave people the license to believe whatever they wanted.

But now relativism is fading because it is not useful.[1] And while it didn't fashion a society free from moral norms, it did buy time until an anti-Christian set of moral norms could be enforced. And that is where we are today. Our culture no longer declares that we all have personal truths. Instead, people are speaking in absolute terms again. There are clearly "right" and "wrong" ways to view a variety of societal issues. Relativism was merely a bridge to take the West from the Christian worldview to another. The bridge has been crossed and relativism is dead.

---

1. There are still pockets of relativism. Consider the last time you went to a Bible study and were asked to share "What [fill in the passage being studied] means to me." Some people do think all religions are the same and equally valid. Some people ask, "Who am I to judge another person's behavior." But even these examples are indications about what people believe to be true more than they are authentic expressions of relativism. The person in the Bible study is guided by beliefs about the nature of Scripture. The person that believes all religions are the same is guided by assumptions about the nature of God and our ability to know Him. And the person that is not quick to judge has already made a judgment that the behavior is not really that bad and so a person should be free to engage in it. This is not relativism. These are convictions about what is true. In these situations, people are making judgments guided by convictions of reality.

Leveraging Relativism's Demise

It may sound surprising to you, but the death of relativism is to our benefit as believers. I don't think we need to convince people anymore that truth exists and that it is absolute. We do not have to fight to persuade society that truth claims should be applied equally to all people. They already affirm this. Do we think it's okay that some people are racists? Do we look the other way when people mistreat others because of their skin color? Do you know anyone who thinks racism is as valid as any other belief? No, our society says it doesn't matter who you are, where you come from, or what your social upbringing was. You are not allowed to be racist. Even if you haven't done anything that counts as racist, you can still be punished if your thoughts come out. With respect to racism, Western society is collectively acting on the belief that it is wrong, always wrong, even fundamentally wrong.

More recently, Western society has decided it is wrong to withhold certain rights from the LGBT community. Legislators are now writing this liberal sexual orthodoxy into law.[2] States and churches are having same-sex marriage forced on them, private business owners face lawsuits if they don't service gay weddings, public schools have gender-neutral restrooms, and teachers teach a curriculum that validates the transgender lifestyle. Western society has rallied around the idea of absolute truth in matters of morality.

This societal sense of fairness is good. The sense of justice is good. It is good to be motivated to act against that which you think is wrong. The land of no morals is worse than the land of misguided ones. America's fight for gay rights shows that people think there is a right way—and a wrong way—to treat people. It shows they recognize the inherent value of personhood and the wrongfulness of denying

---

2. "Orthodoxy" here does not imply the correct way of thinking. The word itself means an authorized or accepted doctrine, belief, or theory—and that is how I am using it. Many have sanctioned a way to view sexuality that is contrary to biblical sexuality; this is what I call "liberal sexual orthodoxy."

rights.[3] These values are good for the gospel because they allow us to raise deeper, more significant questions than who has what rights.

The only basis for human rights and thereby morality is the inherent, ontological value of a person. That is to say, our nature and not our function is the source of our value. People are valuable because they are people. Period. That is why racism is wrong. All people are entitled to be treated with the same level of respect because we all share the same value in our nature, our being. That is it. Personhood alone is the source of value. If personhood were not intrinsically valuable, we wouldn't bat an eye at the sanctioned slaughter of six million Jews. The Holocaust would not be wrong. Neither would rape be wrong, nor slavery. Societies would have the freedom to decide why some people weren't as valuable as others and then arbitrarily use them however they wanted.

But what is the basis for human rights if life merely evolved through a series of fortunate accidents? If life evolved by chance, then it has no ultimate purpose, no ultimate meaning, and no ultimate value. What rights could humans actually possess if life itself never should have happened? "Rights" imply that there are "wrongs." And how can there be wrongs in a universe of no purpose?

But if there is a Creator, there is purpose. And if there is purpose, there can be a fixed and objective value in personhood. Value only makes sense when two things are involved: an object that can possess value and a person who determines value. If humans evolved, they are merely objects that became aware of themselves and pronounced their own value. Our value would then be completely arbitrary, very subjective, and able to change at any time. But if humankind is an object of creation, its value is determined by the One who made it. It can be a fixed value.

---

3. Don't misunderstand my point here. I am not affirming the goodness of homosexuality nor am I affirming the right to same-sex marriage. Rather, I am affirming the goodness of acting to protect people based on a notion of human rights.

Only in the context of theism can life have purpose. And Christianity shows us that purpose. Humans are made in God's image. As His image-bearers, we have a unique capacity to know Him in a relational way. We can experience the fullness of God and His love more than anything else in all of creation. We possess dignity and value because of our nature: God made us in His image. We are valuable because He values us.

Because our value is secured in the nature of God, who is unchangeable, eternal, and good, our value remains constant. God is constant, so our value is constant. Nothing will cause our value to ever diminish. The substitutionary death of Jesus shows us this. His death reflects our innate, constant value. Scripture tells us that while we were still God's enemies, Christ died for us (Rom. 5:1–11). A person can have no greater love than the love that causes them to give up their life. And if Jesus would die for His enemies, it shows that the value He places on us is separate from our actions. Our value is in our nature, that which He came to redeem. The life given to purchase our redemption shows very clearly our value.

Living in the Chaos and the Darkness

If you take people down this road, you will see how humankind's universal sense of justice is to the gospel's advantage. Only one worldview justifies belief in inherent human value and thereby true morality. It is theism. A transcendent creator is needed for our sense of justice to have any value. Existence must have been intentional for life to have intrinsic and objective worth. We can only look at the world and say, "That is wrong!" if there is an eternally fixed "right."

We know this. We just know that humans are valuable because they are people. But why do we know this? How can we justify this belief that people have inherent value? Apart from a creator we can't. That is the hard part for the skeptic. Ask them why people have inherent value if we are the result of time plus matter plus chance. Ask them if they are willing to follow these beliefs to their logical end and live in the chaos and the darkness of a meaningless land. If mankind came from nothing, then all things are permissible. This is not the kind of world anyone wants to live in.[4]

---

4. A special thanks to my good friend Dylan Higgins, author of the Emblem and Lantern series, for helping with the ideas presented in this chapter, and to my editor, Wendy Widder, for making the ideas flow.

Chapter Ten

God

Tonight, instead of discussing the existence or non-existence of God, they have decided to fight for it.
—MONTY PYTHON

Faith and Evidence

I don't mean to fight, but I think God exists and I have good evidence for thinking so. The word "evidence" may seem strange to you, because people often think believing in God takes you into the realm of the unknown, a realm for which we cannot have "proof." We just have to believe. But faith without evidence is foolishness, and the evidence for God and Christianity is good.

In this chapter I want to provide you with a simple and convincing way to explain how you know God exists and why Christianity is the "right" religion. It's the answer I give people when they ask me. It's not very short, but it is simple. It involves three things: the possibility of God's existence, the way He could make Himself known, and the way He has fully made Himself known.

My Answer: Three Steps to the Cross

Most people are not scholars. They are not academics and researchers who have dedicated their lives to a single idea. Furthermore, most
people's objections to God are not intellectual; they are either emotional or volitional.[1] It is not so much their mind but their heart that
rejects God.

The apostle Paul tells us that people know God exists (Rom. 1:18–
23). However, many people suppress this truth. Many believe the
lie that a good life only comes from absolute autonomy. That is to
say, people can only reach their full potential if they break free from
God's "tyrannical" rule. The serpent's lie has deceived many and led
them into rebellion (Gen. 3:1–7), where they cover up the truth of
God's existence with their emotions and intellects. They reject the
truth with their hearts before they suppress it with their minds.

Your role as an apologist, then, is to help them uncover a truth they
already know. But in doing so, you must be careful. Your approach
is just as important as your knowledge. Intellectual discussions will
help some people come back to God, but formal debates should be
reserved for the university and not held in your living room or office.
Your neighbors or coworkers probably do not need a podium and a
moderator to settle the issue about the existence of God. They just
need a good reason to reconsider a truth about God they once believed. Here is how I do it.

1. Establish the possibility of God's existence.

First, I begin by trying to establish a reasonable case for God's
existence. Do not try to prove God exists. All you must do is open
the door for the possibility that He exists. Most people already have
this door open and you can then move on to the next step. However,
if you find someone who is completely closed off to the idea, go back

---

1. Volition refers to one's will.

to the beginning. Ask him how he thinks life came to be. Ask why there is something rather than nothing. Since he doesn't believe in God, he will likely give you a naturalistic answer involving evolution and billions of years.

At this point, don't argue about evolution. Instead, ask what there was in the beginning. Ask if the universe has always existed or if it came from nothing.[2] Ask for evidence. You may get some scientific theories of an eternal universe or dark matter. Likely you will find that your friend is not a scientific expert but is forced to believe this way because of a prior assumption that God does not exist.

Understand that you are not asking these questions to be smug. You are simply trying to expose the level of certainty in your friend's position. What you need is a crack in his defense. Helping your friend see that he doesn't really have good reasons for his beliefs will likely make him more open to yours.

What will probably happen next is that your friend will ask for your evidence. This is good. Chances are you won't be prepared on the spot to present the cosmological,[3] teleological,[4] and natural law[5] arguments for God's existence (though that should be your goal), but you can say, "I would be glad to study it together." Beyond obvious reasons, I suggest you offer to study the evidence for God's existence together because the evidence supports belief in God. If your skeptic friend accepts your invitation, and is an honest, truth-seeking person, he or she will likely become open to the possibility of God's existence. That is all you need in the next step.

---

2. You can point out that it is nonsensical to think that non-existence can bring forth existence as it would first have to exist to bring itself into existence.

3. This argument for God's existence is based on the origin of life.

4. This argument for God's existence is based on the evidence of design in the universe.

5. This argument for God's existence is based on the fact that a universal moral law exists.

2. Consider the way God could make Himself known.

Once you have established that it is at least possible that God exists, the next step is to ask if miracles would be possible. I ask if it would be possible for this God to do things out of the natural order in the world He made. Most people say yes. They understand that if a supernatural being exists, He could do what He wanted in a world He made.

Once they concede the possibility that God and miracles exist, I ask, "Could God use miracles to tell the world who He is?" I ask if it is possible that God would choose to invade the planet He made to let people know who He is. Many people say that it's possible for Him to do this.

3. Examine the way God has made Himself known.

Now the question becomes, *has He?* Has He invaded the planet to make Himself known? There are various miracles that you could refer to in order to convince your skeptic friend of God's existence. But the clincher miracle is the resurrection of Jesus. It not only shows that God exists, but also that Christianity is the right religion. Christianity hangs on the resurrection of Jesus. If the resurrection did not happen, Christianity falls into the mire of man-made religions. But if it did happen, it is reasonable to conclude that God exists and that we can have hope in a heavenly Savior. I recently had a skeptical woman agree with me on this. She said, "The resurrection is kind of the one thing that would seal the deal if it could be proven." I think she is right.

Before I give any evidence for the resurrection, let me make a comment about evidence. I don't want you to think that evidence is all that is needed. I don't want you to think that if you can just present evidence people will believe. First, seeing doesn't equal believing. Remember, people lived with Jesus, saw His miracles, and still did not believe. If people rejected the Son of God to His face, you can expect people to reject Him to yours.

Second, what one person considers good evidence, another will find insufficient. Just ask yourself how you would respond to evidence for UFOs. When people see, hear, or experience something that does not fit in their worldview, they are skeptical. If you do not believe in aliens, you are unlikely to think that a bright light in the night sky is aliens. Similarly, when most adults see a shadow in the corner, they do not assume the bogeyman has come to get them. You likely would not even consider the "evidence" for either aliens or the bogey monster because you have already concluded that neither exists.[6]

Prior beliefs affect how people view evidence and sometimes determine if they will even consider it. This is why evidence is not always compelling. Many people don't allow certain evidence into their courtroom because their worldview discredits it from the start. Because of this, I find it helpful to ask a skeptic what evidence would cause them to believe in God. This question serves two purposes. First, it causes them to be honest with you. From their answer you can deduce if they are genuinely seeking truth or just arguing with you. Second, their answer can help you know what kind of evidence to present. The person may be at a point where "facts" don't matter, and so you can take a soft and compassionate approach, just talking about how Christ has changed your life. Maybe you discover some presuppositions they have about the nature of truth and so you begin there. Perhaps, though, you find they *are* looking for truth, and evidence is what they need.

---

6. Just as many of us would be skeptical of the evidence for monsters and aliens, N. T. Wright and Tim Keller point out that the disciples' worldview would have caused them to have a similar skepticism regarding the bodily resurrection of Jesus. Thomas is the perfect example of this (John 20:24–29). It would have been as difficult for first-century Jews and Gentiles to believe in the bodily resurrection of Jesus as it would be for us today, though for different reasons. See N. T. Wright, *The Resurrection of the Son of God* (Minneapolis: Fortress, 2003), 200–6, and Tim Keller, *The Reason for God: Belief in an Age of Skepticism* (New York: Dutton, 2008), 206–10, for a detailed analysis of this topic.

If they are open to examining evidence, I share the facts that nearly every historian who has studied the resurrection of Jesus accepts.[7] Regardless of their religious convictions, historians agree that Jesus died by crucifixion, His disciples had experiences they believed to be actual appearances of Jesus risen from the grave, and they believed it so strongly that they were killed for preaching the message of Jesus risen.

These facts are important from a historical standpoint because the disciples were early eyewitnesses of Jesus' resurrection and the sincerity of their testimony is corroborated by their painful deaths. People do not suffer for a lie when there is nothing to be gained; none of the apostles recanted their testimony of a risen Jesus, and the only thing they gained was death. The best conclusion to be drawn from these data is that Jesus rose from the grave.[8]

An Example: Finding a Way to Present the Evidence

What I have just described is something you could explain to someone today. It is something that happens to me nearly every week.

---

7. Gary Habermas presents a list of twelve undisputed historical facts: (1) Jesus died by crucifixion; (2) He was buried in a tomb; (3) the disciples were discouraged and fearful for their lives; (4) Jesus' tomb was found empty soon after His burial; (5) the disciples had experiences that they believed were actual appearances of the risen Jesus; (6) due to these experiences the disciples were willing to die for their belief; (7) the proclamation of the resurrection took place very early; (8) the disciples' public testimony and preaching of the resurrection took place in the city of Jerusalem, where Jesus had been crucified; (9) their preaching centered on the death and resurrection of Jesus; (10) Sunday was the day they gathered for worship; (11) James, the brother of Jesus and a skeptic before this time, was converted when he believed he also saw the risen Jesus; (12) just a few years later, Saul of Tarsus (Paul) became a Christian believer due to an experience that he also believed was an appearance of the risen Jesus. See Gary Habermas, *The Risen Jesus & Future Hope* (Lanham, MD: Rowman & Littlefield, 2003), 9–10.

8. The best resources I can recommend on the topic of the resurrection are the works of Gary Habermas and Mike Licona. The evidence presented here can be found in their works in much greater detail. See the topical resource list at the end of this book.

You just need to look for opportunities to steer conversations toward the cross. Here is an example of how I have used this evidence.

Last week I was discussing a sonnet by John Donne with several high school students. (I know you discuss sonnets all the time.) The sonnet by Donne mocked death, comparing it to a sleeping pill. The theme of the sonnet was that death was nothing more than a slave who was used to cause people to fall asleep only to waken unto eternity, and therefore, it should not be feared.

I asked the students if this was a good view of death. They concluded that it was, provided there was life after death. So I asked, "Is there life after death?" Some said yes, and some said no. I asked them how they knew. No one had an answer. So I asked, "Do we just have to have faith one way or the other? Are we just left to wish and hope for an afterlife, or can we know?" This seems like an important question to answer. They agreed.

They asked me what I thought. I told them that I think we can know if there is an afterlife because I think we can know if God exists. They asked me how. I then asked if it was possible that God might exist. All of them said yes. Mind you, in this group of eleven, at least seven are not believers in Jesus; yet all of them agreed that it was possible that God might exist. As I said earlier, this is what most people believe.

After they agreed that God might exist, I asked if this God could do supernatural things in this natural world. I asked if miracles would be possible. They all said yes, every one of them. I asked why they thought miracles could be possible. They explained that if God existed and made the world, He could do what He wanted in it. They agreed that walking on water you created is not really that hard to believe. I said they were smart.

And then I asked, "So, if God exists and could perform a miracle, could He not use a miracle to tell us who He is?" They all responded to my question with a yes. So I asked, "Has He?" They just looked at me, but I could tell that they wanted to know. So I told them about the resurrection of Jesus. I told them that I think the resurrection both tells us that God exists and which religion is the right one. I then told them about the evidence. I explained that virtually all historians who have studied the resurrection believe three things: Jesus died by crucifixion; the disciples believed they saw Him risen; and they died for preaching that He had risen.

I asked how they would explain these facts, how they could explain the rise of Christianity without the resurrection. One student said, "Well, maybe Jesus didn't actually die. Maybe He survived." I said that was a fair idea, but let's talk about it. A theory that Jesus survived the crucifixion would have to involve the following: before Jesus was crucified He was beaten, flogged, forced to carry a cross, and given a crown of thorns to be embedded in His head. We understand what a beating is. We can imagine a crown of thorns, regardless of the size of the thorns. But let's make sure we know what flogging is.

Flogging is when you are whipped by a device that has several leather straps with bone and metal and other sharp objects attached on the ends. Their purpose is to dig into the flesh and rip it off when it is pulled back. It tenderizes and defleshifies you. (They were repulsed at my made-up word "defleshify.") I told them that many men died just from this type of torture alone.

After this torture, Jesus was crucified. Many people are familiar with the crucifixion, but just to be sure that my students had the facts straight, I explained to them that on a cross, a person usually dies by suffocation and how it is excruciating.[9] Hanging on a cross forces your lungs to stop working because the way you hang prevents you from breathing. The only way to breathe is to push up with your feet that have been nailed to the cross. You live as long as you have energy to push up to take a breath, or until they break your legs. Jesus' legs were not broken, but this was how He died on a Roman cross. To

---

9. Death by crucifixion was so painful they invented a word for it: "excruciating," from the Latin meaning "pain of/from crucifixion."

ensure that He was dead, the trained Roman guards stuck a spear in His side.

After Jesus was taken off the cross, He was wrapped in seventy pounds of linen, placed in a dark and damp cave-like tomb, and there He remained for three days.

I told my students that to believe the theory that Jesus survived the cross, you would have to believe that He woke up after three days, unwrapped Himself, folded the linens, rolled away a massive stone, took out a couple of trained Roman guards, walked on nailed-pierced bloody feet, presented Himself to the disciples in this condition, and they said, "You have risen from the grave and are Lord!"

I asked my students, "Does this seem likely?" One responded, "More likely than a resurrection!" I said he was probably right in terms of probability, but then I asked if Jesus arriving in this condition would make the disciples think He was God and perpetuate their preaching of His deity, forgiveness of sins by faith in Him, and a future hope of a resurrected body like His. First-century people were not idiots. They would have known the difference between a resurrection and a survival.

Many students agreed with this assessment. Some did not. One of these asked if it is possible that the disciples just hallucinated. I said that was a fair question and many people hold that view. But then I asked, "Do people share the same hallucination? If you and your friend were 'tripping' would you see the same thing?" He said, "No, and I know." We laughed. Modern psychology agrees with him. Group hallucinations do not happen.

At this point another student chimed in and said, "I think they just made it up!"

So I asked, "You think that the disciples made up that Jesus rose from the grave and then died for their conspiracy for no reason? Why do you think this, do you have any evidence?"

She said, "No, but that's just what I believe."

I encouraged her to base her belief on something more substantial than her opinion because so much is at stake. She said, "Ahhh." Not all stories end well, but hopefully this is not the end of this student's journey to Jesus.

Our group conversation ended with some believing, some being more open to Christianity, and some being exactly as they were before we talked. I encouraged them to have reasons for their beliefs. Much is at stake when it comes to God, and if He exists, you want to know it before you meet Him in the afterlife. I told them that I look forward to future conversations with them.

Your Turn

You can do this. You can talk to people. You can tell them what you know and ask questions. You can even remember the historical evidence for Jesus' death and resurrection. I challenge you to start presenting it. Start driving conversations toward the cross. Begin placing your hope in Jesus to save others. If you are reading this you believe that Jesus can save you from your sins. Why don't you believe He can save others? Open your mouth and let the gospel come out, accompanied by the evidence of His resurrection that you now know.

I encourage you to study and become familiar with the evidence for the resurrection. Most people are surprised to hear that such evidence exists. I have presented the most basic evidence to give you a starting place. But continue to learn and read. At the end of this book, there is a list of excellent sources that can strengthen your faith and equip you to explain your hope and preach the gospel.

Chapter Eleven

Religion

But of course, being a Christian does mean thinking that
where Christianity differs from other religions,
Christianity is right and they are wrong.
—C. S. LEWIS

The Narrow Road

We believe that there is one God. We believe that there is one way
to heaven. And we believe that Jesus is the only way to get to either
of them. We believe there is truth in other religions, but where they
differ from Christianity, they are wrong and Christianity is right. In
our "tolerant" society, these are not acceptable beliefs. Nonetheless,
we must neither back down nor be passive about them.

Narrow is the road that leads to salvation and small is its gate
(Matt. 7:14). Because we love and respect others, we will tell them
this. It is loving to tell people that everlasting life is possible through
Jesus Christ alone. It would be unloving to withhold that truth and
let them walk whatever treacherous path they like. Furthermore, we
respect people by disagreeing with them. Agreeing with everything

someone says is actually a form of condescension. It is what we do with children and the insane. "Oh, you believe fairies make it rain every night? Well, isn't that nice."

Loving people and respecting them involves accepting the risk that comes with telling them they are wrong. But it is the kind of world that we all really want to live in. Imagine the chaos in a world where no one ever pointed out error.

So, despite the claims and wishes of our culture, Christians reject the notion that all religions are the same. Consequently, we are called arrogant, narrow-minded, and judgmental—a funny criticism from people who consider themselves tolerant. Ironically, people who label Christians judgmental for thinking they are right do not consider themselves judgmental for thinking Christians are wrong. What the land of "tolerance" cannot tolerate is Christianity's exclusivity.

Telling people that Jesus is the only way will be met with opposition. It is a deeply engrained lie that "all roads lead to heaven." But all roads don't lead to heaven any more than all roads lead to your house. All religions are not the same. After you have shown that there is good evidence to believe in God, you must be able to tell your friends that Jesus is the only way to Him.

Obviously Different

I think it is obvious to most people that all religions cannot be the same. Most people live in the land of black and white, right and wrong. Most people agree that if I tell you to take a left to get to my house and my wife tells you to go right, one of us is wrong. Likewise, most people understand that if Christians believe there is one God, and Hindus believe that there are millions of gods, and atheists believe that there are no gods, and Mormons believe that you can become a god, then somebody is wrong.

Competing truth claims cannot be equally valid. Earth cannot be both round and flat at the same time. It is possible that competing truth claims are both wrong, but they cannot both be right. The same goes for religion. Opposing religions cannot be equally valid. It is possible that all religions are wrong, but they cannot all be right. Most people know this.

There is some confusion about what it means to say that one religion is right and others are wrong. Saying a religion is wrong is not saying that there is nothing true about it. Religions practice and teach some of the same things. Many share a view of morality, for example; they do not allow murder, rape, lying, and stealing. Many religions do some good in the world. But these similarities do not mean the religions are the same.

Furthermore, why should similarities be more important than differences? The differences matter. For example, some religions have practiced human sacrifice. Are they just as valid and right as those religions that protect human life? Some religions think you can use women however you want because they are less valuable than men. Are they just as right and the same as those that value and cherish women? Do we really want to say that religions which encourage polygamy and the marriage of nine-year-olds are equally as valid as those which protect children? You and your skeptic friend both know the answer to this.

Why Religious Pluralism Is Popular

Even though I think people understand that all religions are not the same, religious pluralism—the belief that all religions are equally valid—is still gaining traction in our society. There are two reasons for this.

First, it's silly to spend time fighting about who would win in a fight between Superman and Batman. And this is what religion is becoming in our society: a fantasy. An entire generation of Christians has grown up knowing little about their religion, much less why it is true.[1] Without this knowledge, the strong religious convictions of

---

1. See "Barna Survey Examines Changes in Worldview Among Christians over

one generation turn into the lightly held assumptions of the next. And religion falls into the category of wishful thinking and fantasy. God is nothing more than the big man upstairs who showers us with gifts if we are good. He is Santa Claus.

Second, religious pluralism is growing because many people have at least one of the following assumptions about God: (1) He cannot be known; (2) He does not care how you live; and (3) He will not hold our ignorance of Him against us. Essentially, people assume that if God is real, He will not be angry with us for not knowing who He is and responding accordingly. They think, *how could a loving God actually send people to hell for not knowing something?* Or as one person put it to me, "So you are telling me that if I get one question wrong on God's test He's going to fail me and send me to a detention with flames? My stupid teachers are more loving than that!" So it doesn't matter which religion you choose. A good God wouldn't care, so neither should we.

But this is a huge assumption with profound implications, and it is itself a religious belief, a giant theological claim that should require evidence for us to believe it. Without such evidence, religious pluralism requires an enormous amount of blind faith.

Logically Impossible

The irony is that if you had evidence that religious pluralism was the "right religion," you would not have religious pluralism. You would have an exclusive religion that had the correct view of God. It is not logically possible for religious pluralism to exist. For example, if it is true that all roads lead to heaven, then Christianity is wrong about its soteriology, its doctrine of salvation. If Christianity is wrong about its defining doctrine, how can it be equally as valid as religions

the Past 13 Years," *Barna Group*, March 6, 2009, https://www.barna.org/barna -update/21-transformation/252-barna-survey-examines-changes-in-world view-among-christians-over-the-past-13-years#.VFl0TPnF-HA.

built on true premises? It can't. That idea is absurd. Whoever heard
of such a thing as right and wrong being equally valid? Therefore, if
Christianity isn't equally as valid as other religions, it undermines
the nature of religious pluralism by showing its main premise—the
equal validity of all religious beliefs—to be false.

The idea of religious pluralism can only exist if you make ignorant assumptions that require an enormous amount of wishful hop-
ing that God will consider sincerity to be as good as accuracy. To be
a religious pluralist, you must hope that God is not like my old—
literally old—high school math teacher. It didn't matter to her that I
got most of a problem right, and that I was genuinely trying. As she
always said, "Ninety percent right equals one hundred percent wrong
in math, sweety."

What Jesus Thinks

Experience and logic show us that all religions are not the same,
and they are not equally valid. One more criterion can help support
these beliefs: Jesus. If Jesus proved He was God by rising from the
dead, wouldn't His perspective on religion be the right one? If Jesus
said there was only one way to heaven, shouldn't we trust Him?

Jesus said there is one path that leads to God and heaven, and it is
narrow: "Enter by the narrow gate. For the gate is wide and the way
is easy that leads to destruction, and those who enter by it are many.
For the gate is narrow and the way is hard that leads to life, and those
who find it are few" (Matt. 7:13–14). These are the words of Jesus, the
man who claimed to be God and died on a cross and rose again. Jesus
claimed that no one can come to God except through Him, that those
who don't believe in Him are condemned and the wrath of God is on
them, and that eternal life is given to those who believe in Him.[2] Jesus
clearly taught an exclusive path to God and heaven.

This leaves skeptics with several options. They can call Jesus a liar;

---

2. John 3:16–19, 36; John 14:6–7.

they can say Jesus was wrong; or they can say the Bible is wrong. People are not likely to go for options one or two. People don't like to call Jesus a liar. And as far as Jesus being wrong, we have already seen that historical evidence supports His resurrection from the dead; since He rose from the grave, affirming that He was divine, I think we can conclude that He would not be wrong about who God is and how to get to Him.

The only reasonable option left is the reliability of Scripture. This is where most skeptics will go. A person could believe that truth exists, that God is knowable, that Jesus died and came back from death, that Christianity is one way to heaven, but think that the Bible is wrong in recording Jesus' teachings on the exclusivity of religion. We will discuss the reliability of the Bible next.

Chapter Twelve

Scripture

Occasionally I see a bumper sticker that reads:
"God said it, I believe it, and that settles it." My response is
always, what if God didn't say it?
—BART EHRMAN

The Attack on the Bible

There was a time in American history when everyone considered the Bible authoritative. That time has passed. People just don't trust the Bible anymore. They have all kinds of questions about it. Some questions are sincere. Some are merely combative. And some are comical. I once talked with a guy who asked, "Who the hell is John, Paul, and the other dude? Did these blokes hang out with Jesus or were they frauds who lived, like, a hundred years after the alleged Jesus died and made up all this BS? John, Luke and—I don't know—Ringo seem to me like fraud people who made up this stuff."

Or take the friend of mine who thinks the Bible is full of contradictions. He walked into my office one morning and the first thing out of his mouth was, "I'm mad at the Bible!"

I laughed and said, "What did it do to you this time?"

He replied, "Why is it that nobody can get straight what the last words of Jesus were? You would think that they would have gotten something that important right, but they all say something different about what Jesus' last words were." He wasn't kidding when he said he was mad at the Bible. He was very angry that morning.

You probably have your own stories for this discussion. You likely have met someone who has a problem with the Bible. The question before us in this chapter is what to say to that person. Do we have to be able to prove to people that the Bible is the inspired and inerrant Word of God?[1] Does a person have to "believe in" the Bible to be saved? These are questions we need to think about because people sometimes use their objections to the Bible as reasons not to believe in God. We must be prepared to answer their objections because their view of the Bible is not a good enough reason to dismiss God.

A Separate Issue

I don't let skeptics avoid the topic of God by dismissing the Bible. The Bible is a separate discussion, and although it is an important discussion, it is not foundational to belief in God's existence. Simply put, when a person tells you that they don't believe in the Bible, you should ask, "So?" Ask what belief in the Bible has to do with God's existence. You can point out that even if the Bible is false, God could still be real. Strictly speaking, the fate of the Bible is not related to the fate of God. You cannot dismiss the Bible and think that will get rid of God.

Although the Bible is not essential for belief in God, an obvious question is, "Well, if the Bible isn't reliable, how do Christians know they are right about things like God and salvation?" That's a great question. But notice, I have not told the skeptic that the Bible isn't

---

1. "Inspired" means "God-breathed," which Christians understand to mean God wrote the Bible through human authors; and "inerrant" means without any mistakes.

reliable, that it's a forged or inaccurate book about God and related matters. I have simply made a point that forces the skeptic to keep talking with me. This is a strategy I use to keep the conversation going by removing an unnecessary obstacle.

I say strategy, but don't misunderstand me. It is not a gimmick on my part to say that the Bible could be a man-made, mistake-filled book and God would still exist. This is a true statement. It is a true statement that disarms many skeptics. It removes what they consider a secret weapon in their arsenal of objections. Once they are disarmed, we can profitably talk about the reliability of the Bible.

The Main Issue

I do not argue for the inerrancy of the Bible with skeptics and I will not be arguing for it in this chapter. This is not because I do not believe the Bible is inerrant, but because debates on the inerrancy of the Bible should be had among Christians. They are not necessary in the battle for people's hearts, minds, and souls.

The Bible *could* contain mistakes and we would still be assured of our salvation. Therefore, you do not need to defend the inerrancy of Scripture with skeptics. They can be saved without it. Don't muddle your evangelism with unnecessary debates that are hard to win.

The reliability of the Bible is not a hard debate to win. Besides death and taxes, the historical reliability of the Bible is one of the most certain things in life. Despite objections you hear from friends, snippets you watch on the History Channel, or titles of books you see on the best-seller rack, the Bible is the most reliable ancient document in the world. I say this not from a Christian perspective, but from a literary and historical one. The reliability of the Bible is so great that if we dismiss it as untrustworthy, we have to dismiss all other ancient documents.[2] In terms of historical reliability, the Bible is in a class by itself.

---

2. See Josh McDowell, *Evidence That Demands a Verdict*, vol. 1 (Nashville: Thomas Nelson, 1999), 15–74.

When we talk about the reliability of the Bible, we are not talking about one book. We are talking about a collection of books written over a 1,500-year span of time by more than forty authors in three languages. Most people don't know this. When they say they don't believe the Bible, they think they are rejecting one book written by one person at one point in history. It is an understandable mis-understanding. The majority of world religions owe their religious texts to a single person. This is one of the things that make the Bible so unique. Make sure your skeptic friend is aware of this. You don't get to dismiss the Bible in one swoop. You have to dismiss sixty-six individual books written by different people at different times.

You do not have to defend all sixty-six books. What I do is defend twenty-seven of them, and so create a good reason to accept all of them. I focus on defending the reliability of the New Testament. This is for two reasons.

First, I think the biggest concern you should have with a skeptic is to convince them of the resurrection of Jesus.[3] Don't get sucked into a discussion about worldwide floods or people living in whales. You can deny the flood and Jonah's time in the whale and still be saved. I recommend that you not waste your energy fighting these battles.

A second reason to argue just for the reliability of the New Testa-ment is that proving the general reliability of the New Testament also proves the general reliability of the Old Testament. The New Testa-ment includes Jesus' affirmation of the Old Testament. Jesus teaches the Old Testament as the Word of God, so if the New Testament is reliable, we can also trust the Old Testament.[4] Let's consider the evi-dence for the reliability of the New Testament.

---

3. An excellent resource to help you with this is Gary R. Habermas and Michael R. Licona, *The Case for the Resurrection of Jesus* (Grand Rapids, MI: Kregel, 2004).

4. See, for example, Matt. 5:17–18; Mark 12:26; Luke 16:17; 24:44; John 10:35.

Is the New Testament Reliable?

Judging the reliability of an ancient document begins with asking how many copies of the document are available to us. Original manuscripts of ancient documents do not exist; writing materials are too easily destroyed. So copies of ancient documents are as good as it gets, but copies are sufficient.

Copies can be used to reconstruct the text of an original manuscript. This process is called textual criticism. The more copies you have, the easier it is to sort through copying errors and determine the original text. Here is an example of how you can reconstruct an original text from four hypothetical copies of Phil. 4:13:[5]

1. I can do all t#ings through Christ who strengthens me.
2. I can do all th#ngs through Christ who strengthens me.
3. I can do all thi#gs through Christ who strengthens me.
4. I can do all thin#s through Christ who strengthens me.

In this example, it's very easy to tell that the original text said, "I can do all things through Christ who strengthens me." This is how you reconstruct an original manuscript from its copies. You can see that the more copies you have, the more certainty you can have that the reconstruction is accurate.

So how many copies of the New Testament do we have? There are more than 25,000 manuscripts in existence today, and nearly 6,000 of them are in Greek, the original language of the New Testament. Nearly 600 of these were copied within the first thousand years of the originals. The oldest Greek manuscript of the New Testament, a fragment from John's gospel, dates to the early second century—mere decades from the original. By comparison, there are fewer than 2,000 manuscripts of the closest competitors, the Homeric epics, *Illiad* and

---

5. Norman L. Geisler and Frank Turek use this example in their book *I Don't Have Enough Faith to Be an Atheist* (Wheaton, IL: Crossway, 2004), 228.

Odyssey. The oldest Homeric manuscript is about 350 years removed from the original.[6]

The New Testament leads the way when it comes to manuscript reconstruction. It is well ahead of the pack. New Testament manuscripts are the most numerous and earliest of all ancient documents by far. There is little doubt that we have the correct version of the New Testament. Even some of the most critical adversaries of the Bible agree that the New Testament we have today contains the original beliefs of Christianity.[7]

Is the Bible Truthful?

Because we have such a high degree of assurance that we have the correct version of the New Testament, the only question remaining for us is if the original writers told the truth. Did the writers of the New Testament invent their stories? Were they accurate in what they wrote about Jesus and His teachings? How would we know? Just knowing we have an accurate copy of the New Testament is not enough. It could just be an accurate copy of a lie.

We have good reason to believe the New Testament authors told the truth because their writings meet certain historical tests. I will explain two. First, the New Testament exhibits the characteristics of truthful eyewitness accounts. For example, the New Testament eyewitness testimony includes embarrassing details about its authors. If you were to lie, would you craft a lie that makes you look bad? The

---

6. These statistics are from an e-mail correspondence with New Testament textual critic Daniel Wallace (June 12, 2014). The number of manuscripts continues to grow. Before this book goes to press, the statistics here will be out of date! One of the more fascinating recent findings has been the discovery of manuscripts in Egyptian burial masks. Burial masks are essentially papier-mâché. Through a delicate procedure, the masks are able to be taken apart and hundreds of new manuscripts have been found, including Greek poetry and New Testament fragments.

7. See Bart Ehrman, *Misquoting Jesus* (New York: HarperSanFrancisco, 2005), 252.

eyewitness testimony also includes the testimony of women, and in the first century women were not considered reliable sources. Would you create a lie that includes a witness that you knew no one would trust? The New Testament also contains the testimony of martyrs. Would you create a lie that would get you killed? At the very least, would you not recant when a sword is at your neck?[8]

Second, the New Testament records events to which multiple independent sources attest. Remember, the New Testament is not one book. It is a collection of independent sources that often speak about the same thing. The principle here is that the more sources you have recording the same event, the higher the level of certainty that the event happened. We also have extra-biblical sources, some of which were written by enemies of Christianity, corroborating key details of the New Testament.[9]

The Bigger Picture

The New Testament passes every test the historian can throw at it. I have kept my explanation short, but I encourage you to study this further. You will meet people who want you to explain more than what I have offered. The good news is that, although I have been brief, it is not for lack of evidence. You will have no problem finding answers to skeptics' questions about the Bible.

Let me give you the bigger picture to help you move past people's objection to the reliability of the Bible to the reason for the objection. Most people haven't studied the Bible or its reliability. They say they don't believe the Bible because it helps justify their rejection of God. But you can use what they think about the Bible to expose the deeper issue of their unbelief.

---

8. See Geisler and Turek, *I Don't Have Enough Faith to Be an Atheist*, 230–97.
9. See Craig L. Bloomberg, "Jesus of Nazareth: How Historians Can Know Him and Why It Matters," *The Gospel Coalition*, Nov. 5, 2014, http://legacy.the gospelcoalition.org/publications/cci/jesus_of_nazareth_how_historians_ can_know_him_and_why_it_matters.

I began this chapter talking about my friend who was "angry at the Bible." At the end of our conversation, I asked him, "You have a problem that the Gospel writers say something different here, correct?"

"That's right."

"Would you also have a problem if the four Gospels were identical to each other?"

"Yeah, if they were identical it would be a good indication that the writers got together and made it up."

"So you are angry because there are differences, but you would be angry if the books were all the same?"

"Uh-huh," he said.

He saw his problem. I pounced on his honesty and asked him, "Are you sure you have a problem with the Bible? It seems that your problem is that you *want* to have a problem with the Bible."

After a moment he said, "You know, you're right."

This was the biggest breakthrough I had with this friend. He was able to see that he was not interested in whether God existed. He was trying to find ways to reject Him. There is a difference. Help your friends see this. Ask them if they are seeking truth or trying to justify what they already believe. Discussions on the Bible are an excellent opportunity to do this.

Chapter Thirteen

Evil and the Problem of Pain

*If God is all good and all powerful, why does He allow evil to
exist and bad things to happen to good people?*
—EVERY PERSON WHO HAS EVER EXISTED

A Roadblock of Pain

By now you should be able to explain why it's reasonable for
Christians to hope in Jesus Christ. We know that truth exists, and
we can know the God who revealed it. This God revealed Himself in
Jesus, who, according to good historical evidence and reliable written
accounts in the Bible, rose from the dead. I hope you have seen that
there is more to Christianity than wishful thinking, and I hope you
feel more comfortable to share your faith with others.

Now I want to equip you to respond to a common objection to
God: the problem of pain. Simply put, the problem of pain is the belief that an all-good, all-powerful God would not allow bad things
to happen to good people. If He's really God, He should destroy evil.
That He doesn't makes people wonder if He even exists—and if He
does, why would they want to know Him?

Evil and the problem of pain is a subject that requires gentleness and sincerity. A grieving, hurting person does not need lofty, intellectual answers. The problem of pain is a serious and difficult issue for many people to get past. Evil is real, and really bad things have happened to people who didn't deserve it.

It does no good to say that we are all bad and deserve what we get. We are sinners, and we do deserve separation from God and punishment for our sins. But none of this means that a four-year-old girl deserves to be cruelly abused by her father. It does not mean that a village of subsistence fishermen deserves to be wiped off the map by a tsunami. It does not mean that a vibrant young mother deserves to die from cancer before her children reach middle school. Evil is real, really bad things have happened to good people, and it is cruel to suggest that people deserve everything that happens to them. Profound personal tragedy causes real, emotional reactions against God and belief in Him.

Others use the problem of pain as an intellectual reason to reject Christ. They believe that if God were actually all-good and all-powerful as Christians claim, He would both want and be able to destroy evil. But evil exists. Therefore, either God is not good or He is not powerful enough to get rid of it. Either way, He isn't a God to be worshiped. And more likely, He simply doesn't exist.

Clearing the Roadblock

You must discern whether a person's struggle with the problem of evil is emotional or intellectual. The nature of their objection determines how you approach it. In my experience, the problem of pain is most often an emotional roadblock that prevents a person from coming to Christ,[1] so we will address this position first.

The best place to start is by expressing genuine concern for a

---

1. Gary Habermas thinks that most doubts are emotional in nature. Habermas, "Emotional Doubt" (lecture, National Apologetics Conference, Charlotte, NC, October 28, 2011).

person's pain. Do not dismiss someone's grief by offering such lofty, thoughtless statements as "God moves in mysterious ways." A mother who has lost a child will want nothing to do with a God whose mysterious ways include sitting back and watching children suffer.

Don't pretend to know the mind of God. I would not even tell a grieving person that God must have a plan. God's plan isn't very important to someone who's engulfed by grief. I understand that these remarks are usually well-intentioned and meant to give hope, but they don't. Mostly, they just hurt. Worse, they alienate you from the very person you are trying to comfort and help.[2]

The best thing you can do is offer comfort. Comfort can lead to hope, and hope can lead to an understanding of purpose. You don't know why God allows some bad things to happen, and it's better not to pretend you do. But there actually is comfort in that fact that God is the kind of God who allows bad things to happen to good people: if God did not allow bad things to happen to good people, He never would have allowed Jesus, an innocent and good man, to suffer and die on the cross, and we would be of all people most to be pitied (1 Cor. 15:19). I am grateful that God allowed the worst evil possible to come upon the best person ever—for no wrongdoing of His own.

This is comforting because, though I may not understand why God does not prevent more pain on earth, I know that He Himself has experienced the deepest pain. More importantly, His pain made the way for us to be saved from pain forever. It comforts people to know that God knows pain. In such comfort, they will be more likely to see that God uses pain for good. Hope is found in knowing that pain is not necessarily gratuitous.[3]

---

2. Telling a grieving Christian that God has a plan *may* be of some value (though it's usually better simply to say, "I'm so sorry for your loss," and then stop talking), but we are referring here to people who have yet to come to Christ.

3. Pain in general is not unnecessary, and pain itself is a good thing. It often protects us from worse harm. A child who has burned a finger on a hot stove is less likely to touch it again.

Jesus knows better than we do what pain is like, and because of His pain, He holds the keys to infinite happiness and the deed to a future land free of evil. Jesus walked through the valley of suffering, was subjected to the cruelty of evil men, and bought my freedom with His pain. So when I am in pain, I know that my God knows my pain firsthand. I can rest in that. I can take comfort from the One who has been where I am.

Directing One's Anger

It is good to acknowledge the appropriateness of anger in the midst of evil and pain. It is right to be angry over injustice. It is right to be sick about crimes against children. It is good for you to feel a hole in your stomach when you see the devastation and loss of life caused by a natural disaster. It is right to think, "This is not how life is supposed to be." The key is to direct anger at the right thing so that you follow the right path of action.

Anger is a motivating force. It pushes us into action. Anger is a powerful emotion and so we must be careful with it. But when you are angry for the right reasons—and angry at the right thing—your righteous anger can lead you to do good things. Being angry at sin is good because it can cause people to seek its remedy, Jesus. And this is your role. Help people direct their anger at the appropriate object: sin.

Acknowledging a person's sense of justice can help lead them to repentance. When we are angry at evil, we are acknowledging that life has purpose. We are recognizing that there is a difference between good and bad. We are affirming that bad should be punished. But if bad should be punished, what does that mean for my own bad behavior? And where did I get my sense of justice in the first place? If life is an accident, how can it have purpose? And if life has no purpose, why am I angry at what I think is unfair? My sense of the way things ought to be indicates that I believe in a standard of life.

But what standard? Whose standard? A standard merely made by society? That can't be. That would be entirely too arbitrary. It would mean that the Holocaust wouldn't have been wrong because the Nazis' actions were in line with the standard they created. It would mean that a society of pedophiles could create a standard to reflect their urges. No, we understand the folly in this line of thinking.

So, when I am angry at evil I recognize that life's purpose has been violated. But who established life's purpose? This is the right question to ask. And your anger can lead you to ask it. People's sense of justice can point them to the good Judge. When you talk with people who are angry at pain and evil, affirm their outrage and direct it properly. Leverage their moral indignation and use it to reconcile them to the moral lawgiver. Let their anger over sin send them to the Creator, Sustainer, and Savior of life.

The Intersection of Freedom and Evil

Some people will raise an intellectual response to their emotional pain and say, "Why did it have to be this way? Why didn't God just create a world where people could feel no pain and do no wrong? We wouldn't be able to hurt other people, and if we couldn't sin, then Jesus wouldn't have had to die." This is a fair question to ask, but let's consider what such a place would really be like. It would have to be a place where freedom did not exist. It would have to be a place where we didn't have the ability to choose. Quite simply, in this world, you could never make a decision because it might be a bad one that results in pain. Something as simple as walking would have to be controlled by a force other than your will. You could step in a hole and twist an ankle. You could take the wrong trail, get lost, and freeze alone in a cold forest. No, you couldn't make any decisions. You would have to be made like a robot or a tree and simply do what you were made to do.

This type of world would not be worth creating by a good God.[4] If

---

4. In fact, you might argue that God couldn't create this kind of world because it would be in conflict with His holy nature. To create this kind of world, God

pain were eliminated because decisions were eliminated, things like love and friendship would be eliminated as well. Love does not come by force; it is discovered by creatures who choose to give it or reject it. But with the ability to choose to love comes the ability to choose to hate. The greater potential something has for good, the greater potential it has to become evil. Freedom is both good and dangerous.

Therefore, either we exist as robots, incapable of enjoying the few things that make life worth living, or we exist with the ability to make decisions, some of which will cause pain. You cannot have it both ways.[5] The all-wise God considered it worth the risk to create a world in which evil could exist so that things like love could exist too. Considering this, it is difficult to argue about what should have been with the Being who gave you the freedom to argue.

The Intersection of Sin, Pain, and Goodness

Evil exists largely because people are free to make decisions, some of which will be bad. For God to remove evil He would have to remove freedom. I think this is a fair answer to the question of why God allows evil, but it does not address why He allows the pain that comes from things like cancer or hurricanes or birth defects. I'm not sure I have the most satisfying answers, but I can offer you two.

First, some pain is caused by the intersection of two or more good things. God has created an intricate world with a host of things needed for good to take place. Throwing a baseball with my son in the park is a good thing and requires things such as air and gravity

---

would be doing a bad thing: enslaving people. He would be creating a world in which He was the grand tyrant and not a benevolent father.

5. I am not trying to get mired in the debate over election and free will in this section. That is above my pay grade, as they say. I firmly acknowledge both God's sovereignty and our volitional freedom. I think each are taught in Scripture. I do not fully understand how they relate to one another, though I am certain that God is not held hostage by our freedom. That is to say, God does not cater to us and our free decisions nor is He bound by them.

and matter. This is all good, except when another person freely enjoying a nice walk that day crosses the path of the ball. The collision of good things has inflicted pain. This is inevitable in a free world. Sometimes good things result in pain because of our inability to see perfectly the effects of our decisions. And this extrapolated out to more severe circumstances can give some explanation to the pain that exists in life.[6]

Second, much of our pain is the natural consequence of sin in a good, but fallen, world. Christianity says that our sin has affected all of God's creation, including our bodies. It acts like a disease and ruins what God created good. As far as the power of sin goes, God dealt with it on the cross of Jesus. Sin may be allowed to wreak havoc now, but this does not mean it will always be able to. Because of Jesus, we have hope that the mess we've made of this present world will be cleaned up. And for that we wait earnestly.

The Problem of Pain Is a Problem for Skeptics

In this section, I want to consider how to respond to people who consider the problem of evil from a purely intellectual position. It is not a personal tragedy that causes them to question God's existence; it is simply their philosophical claim that evil and God cannot exist together.

---

6. Another example is the effect of technology on the world. Using our minds is good. Creating to solve problems is good. The invention of the cell phone was good. Using it to call the ambulance when you need help is good. But what is the effect of technology on our environment? Could the cell phone that helps save life also be a cause for harm? What is the full impact of the cell phone's radiation on our bodies, a developing fetus, or our environment? This is not information that we can have perfectly. Time is needed to see how things fully relate to each other. But even with time I don't think it is possible to examine fully the way technology affects our environment because new technology is always being created, changing the variables. Our limited knowledge makes it impossible to see all the consequences of good things interacting with each other.

Those who reject God out of personal pain focus on the "why question": why does God allow evil? Those who reject God from an intellectual position are more forceful: God (as we know Him) and evil cannot exist together. This argument assumes that since God is supposed to be all-good and all-powerful, He would want to be rid of evil and would therefore get rid of it. The logical conclusion is that since evil obviously exists, God must not.

There are at least two major problems with this position. The first is the relationship between choice and evil. Much of this world's evil results from people's actions. If the world is to be rid of evil, it must also be rid of morally free creatures. So there is no contradiction in an all-good, all-powerful God allowing evil to remain (unless we think a good God should enslave us).

The second problem with this argument is our ability to identify something as evil at all if God does not exist. When we say that something bad has happened, we are saying that something has happened in a way that things should not happen. We are saying something is wrong. We are not simply saying that something has happened in a way that we personally do not like, such as being served a steak well done when you prefer it rare. Rather, we instinctively know that evil is something beyond our personal taste. People universally understand, for example, that it is not just that we *prefer* people not murder each other. We think it is fundamentally wrong. But where did everyone get this idea of wrong?

If something happens accidentally, it has no purpose. This does not mean it cannot come to have a purpose, but the purpose would be decided individually and independently. For example, say a man finds a rock that has broken off of a bigger rock by chance. He decides to use it for a hammer. The rock now has purpose, but it very well could have been used for a thousand other things. It was not created for any specific purpose, thus there is no right or wrong way to use it.

Likewise, if God does not exist, if He did not create life, then life is the result of randomness; it is an accident without specific purpose.

And if life has no purpose, then there is not a right or wrong way things should be. There is no way to use life wrongly, because life itself is an accident. Even if people assign purpose to life, they are still just acting like the man who found the fallen rock and gave it a random purpose when it could have had another. It is an arbitrary purpose, without any real significance, and what significance it does have is not binding.

Yet when it comes to evil, everyone says that somewhere life is being used wrongly. We call molestation evil because we believe children should not be used that way. We call racism evil because we believe people should not be judged on the basis of their skin color. We call the torture of innocent people for pleasure disgusting and pure evil because we believe no one should use another person's pain for personal satisfaction. We call the Holocaust evil because we believe no one should use their power to destroy people they don't like.

But why should things be one way and not another if life is an accident? The word "should" here is problematic for the skeptic. Why *should* you not steal? Why *should* you not rape? Why *should* you not murder? Why *should* you not treat people based on the color of their skin? The problem of evil is actually a greater problem for skeptics than it is for Christians, because without God, there is no good answer to why we should do one thing and not another.

Ask skeptics these questions, wait for their answer, and you will see the problem of their position. They will be forced to say something is wrong either because it hurts others or because it doesn't benefit society, which is really the same answer. But why is it wrong to hurt others? Why is it wrong for me to do things that benefit me and not society? Who cares if society goes to hell as long as I am fine? Who says hurting people is a bad thing? Who's to say that I can't consider something good if it helps me? How can the skeptic say otherwise?

The skeptic will likely go back to saying that hurting others is wrong because it doesn't benefit society, and a functioning and safe society is to everyone's advantage. But, again, what if I prefer to live in a society that is unsafe where I can take whatever I want? How can you tell me that your way of thinking is more correct than mine, and furthermore, why "should" I prefer your society to mine? To what standard of rightness are you appealing? You cannot simply say that I shouldn't be selfish because it doesn't answer the question of why I shouldn't be selfish. And if the answer is that my unselfishness benefits society, we are right back where we started (thank you, C. S. Lewis, for that last bit of wisdom[7]).

If life just happened, as the skeptic says, then there is no way things *should* be. And if there is no way things should be, every rule we have made is according to personal preference. It may be true that people prefer to live without fear of their possessions being taken, and even if a majority of people prefers this, it is completely different from it being wrong. Wrongness implies a violation of something's intended purpose, not just group preferences. Without a transcendent standard of what is right, there is no way a skeptic can argue that I "should" do anything.

Contrary to what the skeptic says, we know that evil is more than just an infraction of man-made rules and preferences. We understand that evil violates something sacred and ancient that we had no hand in making. Furthermore, we know that even if people decided to legalize the torture of innocent people, it would still be evil. We know that there is a certain way that life is supposed to be. We just know it.

But how can life have any meaning and purpose without a creator? Purpose does not happen by accident; it can only come to be on purpose. The idea of evil only makes sense in a universe of purpose that contains a standard of goodness. We call things evil when they violate this standard. But this standard is not a result of random selection or accident. Accidents are not binding. No, this standard

---

7. C. S. Lewis, *Mere Christianity* (Macmillan Paperbacks Edition; New York: Macmillan, 1960), 26–30.

must have come from a being outside creation who had an intention for life. This being is God. He, Himself, is the standard of goodness.

Even though the problem of evil and pain is a serious issue, it is an issue that helps prove God's existence. With love and compassion, help people see this. Use the problem of pain to gently lead people to the God who loves them, has created good things, and will entirely free them from pain one day.

Part Four

Where You Go

Chapter Fourteen

The World

How much do you have to hate somebody to believe that
everlasting life is possible and not tell them that?
—PENN JILLETTE

Go

Will you go? Will you do more than just learn? Will you act on your desire to persuade others that Jesus is the Messiah? You need to wrestle with this. You need to decide if you are going to be someone who takes our Lord's mercy and grace to others or if you are going to be someone who hoards it. I am pleading for an active evangelism. Christianity is a going religion, not a sitting one. We don't wait for the world to come to us. We go.

We don't rest on the grace of Jesus and use it as cushion for our pews. We don't cherish the love of God, wrapping ourselves in it while looking out the window where people are freezing to death. We are not people who gather on Sunday so that our church leaders can stick pacifiers in our mouths and rock us to sleep, singing soft easy words in our ears.

Or are we?

Some troubling trends exist in the West, and a weak brand of Christianity is one of them. For many professing Christians, it is enough to sing about the wonderful cross rather than picking it up. It is enough to jump from church to church looking for someone to feed us spiritual food, while we neglect the truly hungry. The luxury of prosperity and freedom has made us soft and selfish. We view our religion as an end unto itself. Church programs build more church programs and we hire more staff to support them. "Bring the world to us" we think. And as churches grow in size, the Christian voice becomes fainter and fainter in the West. Our impact is greatly disproportionate to our size. Our religion is for us and our good alone. The rest of the world can go to hell.

But let this not be so any longer. Sin is ruining lives. It causes many people great pain. The world is seeking peace and rest, and they are not finding it. True rest and peace come from Jesus alone. Only the forgiveness of sins brings rest. We know this.

We have lived in the folly of sin. We have run from Jesus, trying to find freedom on our own—only to find bondage instead. Once upon a time, we bore sin's yoke. But we have seen the true nature of that master. He is not gentle or humble, and his yoke is not easy. We have experienced the deceitful nature of sin.

And still, many of us have forgotten. It is easy for us to forget the reality of sin's power. We get caught up in our Christian subculture and forget how much sin robs and steals and kills. We have faithfully abided in Christ and obeyed His teaching, and we have been blessed and protected from much of the hurt that is out there. And this is good. I am glad that faithfully following Jesus results in a wellness. I am grateful for joy and peace and freedom in Christ. I am glad that the joy and peace of Jesus can make it hard to remember the depth of pain from a previous life. Further, I am glad knowing that faithfully following Jesus protects my children from some unnecessary pain. Surely it does not preclude all pain, but following Jesus avoids the worst kind of pain—pain that results from your own stupid, foolish sin.[1] But I must not forget what it was like to live in that place apart from Jesus. And I must not forget those who still live there. I must go.

Paul's Evangelism

Paul went. He went because he considered something greater than his own comfort (Phil. 3:8). He did not count his life of any value, but only hoped that he could accomplish the ministry the Lord gave him (Acts 20:24). He so desired the good of others that he would take their pain upon himself if possible (Rom. 9:3). Paul's evangelism gives us a blueprint to follow and a motivation to embrace.

Paul's evangelistic style was quite simple, simple enough that you could begin implementing it into your life today. That's not to say that there won't be any work involved, but the way Paul shared the gospel is something we all can do.

The basis of Paul's evangelism is that it was active and intentional. He never accidentally shared his faith. I've heard a lot of teaching about evangelism, and sometimes it's presented with an "as you go" mentality: as you go through your normal routine, take the gospel. To be sure, this ought to happen. But if you do not plan to share the gospel, you will never seize opportunities when they come. You will never even see them. We are not inclined to see something we are not looking for. But if your plan is to share the gospel, you will see opportunities everywhere.

You know what I am talking about. You have decided that it is time to get a new car, so you start looking. You research and test drive and hunt down the best price. You finally land on the particular car you want to buy, and suddenly the road is filled with them. You never noticed them before, but now they are everywhere.

---

1. There is a practical, pragmatic nature of obedience. The Lord created all. He knows best how life should be lived. When we obey Him, we avoid the pain that often follows disobedience.

So it is with evangelism. When you are not looking for opportunities to share the gospel, you never see them. But when evangelism is your plan, the field is plentiful and the harvest is ripe. Evangelism cannot only be opportunistic. It cannot only happen by happenstance, because only when you are intentional will you see and seize opportunities. That was Paul's approach.

The Model

In Acts 17, we see a very full picture of what Paul's evangelistic practices looked like. We see his intentionality, his flexibility, and his cultural sensitivity. Specifically, we see a model for us to follow: Go often to people you know well and be prepared to seize opportunities along the way.

Go often.

In the second verse of Acts 17 there are four words, profound words that are easily passed by: "As was his custom." When Paul came to a new city, he went first to the synagogue and would stay as long as he was welcome. Week after week, he would go until he was run off. Why is this significant? The brilliance of Paul's evangelism is in its practicality.[2]

What happens when you do the same thing over and over again? Proficiency. Routine brings proficiency. Many of us are bad at sharing the gospel because we go months or years between the times we engage in evangelism. And, moreover, the last time we shared was likely a completely different context, offering little help for a present opportunity.

---

2. There were also personal and theological reasons for Paul going to the synagogue first. Paul was motivated by his heritage and understanding of God's plan of salvation throughout history. First, he loved his fellow Jews, his brothers. He desperately wanted his family to know freedom in Christ. Second, Paul saw how Israel played a role in God's historical redemptive purposes. Meaning, God has always used Israel in bringing redemption to the world and God is still using Israel in this way (see Rom. 9–11).

What was gained by Paul going to the same place over and over again? What can be gained by following his model? When you go to the same place repeatedly, you often get to know the people well and you'll have more than one opportunity to share the gospel. You have time to think about their questions, and you become more articulate in your presentation. You simply become more comfortable with the process. You are not thrown off by hard questions. You know how to handle an angry person. And, perhaps most importantly, you learn a person's particular stumbling block to faith.

Go to people you know.

The Jews stumbled over the idea of a suffering messiah. Paul knew this. He knew they thought the Messiah would be a conquering king, not a suffering servant. He also knew how to get them past this road-block (Acts 17:3). Paul was a Hebrew of Hebrews and a Pharisee when it came to the law (Phil. 3:4–6). He had been at the top of his field among Jewish religious leaders. Who was more equipped to be able to reason with them from the Scriptures, proving that Jesus was the Messiah who had to suffer? Paul's past uniquely enabled him to understand the way Jews thought and to lead them to repentance and faith in Jesus. Like Paul, your own life experience enables you to understand well what keeps a particular group of people from Jesus. You are uniquely qualified to help them get past it. Start thinking about who the Lord has already prepared you to go to because of your past.

Communication is much easier when you have something in common. Perhaps you are an athlete and you know athletes well. You know what makes them tick. You speak their language. You know their struggles, desires, and ambitions. You know better than anyone else how to connect with them. You are well suited to help them overcome their objections to faith in Jesus.

It need not be complicated. I am a father. I know fathers. I am qualified to help fathers come to Christ. It is easy for me to talk to fathers:

we have at least one thing in common to talk about. Practicing Paul's style of evangelism, I just need to go find fathers and be where they are often. So I go to parks and, like Paul, I go often because inevitably I see the same people from week to week. I put myself in places where I can regularly interact with people I understand.

In my city, parks are the best place for me to go. I live in an outdoor community, and people are always at one of our many parks—willing to talk. For you, it may be the local coffee house or ball field. You might have a downtown area with lots of shops and a casual atmosphere. You just need to identify the best place to find and talk to the people you naturally connect with and be intent on sharing the gospel.

The trick then is directing conversations toward the cross. This is a skill you develop the more you do it. For me, it is easier than it is for most people because I have an advantage: I am a pastor. I have the luxury of just asking what someone does for a living to get the conversation moving toward Jesus. People then ask what I do, and our conversation is headed toward the cross.

The more you practice evangelism, the more you will find ways to direct conversations. It can be as easy as asking someone where they go to church. The hardest part of evangelism is opening my mouth with gospel intentions. Once I conquer that, the battle of what to say usually takes care of itself.

Seize opportunities.

Paul intended to share the gospel, and then he seized opportunities when they came. After Paul was run out of Thessalonica and Berea in Acts 17, he went to Athens. While he was waiting there, "his spirit was provoked within him as he saw that the city was full of idols. So he reasoned in the synagogue with the Jews and the devout persons, and in the marketplace every day with those who happened to be there" (Acts 17:16–17).

Notice that while Paul was waiting his spirit was provoked. Waiting implies a break in a plan. When there is no schedule there is no waiting. Sensitivity to the Spirit's leading is characteristic of those who are already going. You will not sense the Spirit's leading to go to people you don't know if you are not already going to people you do know. Opportunity does not come to the sluggard. It passes him while his eyes are closed.

The Lord put Paul in a time of waiting, an interruption in his evangelistic plans. This waiting turned into a blessing for Paul and for the Athenians. Times of waiting are divinely ordered. They are unique times for God to work His good plan. Embrace them and do not lose heart in them. Cultivate eyes and a heart for the lost, and when the Lord stops you in your tracks seize the opportunity for the gospel.

If you read further in Acts 17, you will see that Paul's response to the prompting of the Spirit gave him an opportunity to speak at the Areopagus (Acts 17:19). This was not part of Paul's plan, and the audience at the Areopagus was not a Jewish audience. Notice what Paul did at the Areopagus: in the synagogue, he had reasoned from the Scriptures, proving that Jesus was the Messiah, but in Athens, he quoted Greek philosophers and poets. He spoke to his audience in a language they would understand (Acts 17:28).[3] Jews recognized the authority of Scripture. Epicurean and Stoic philosophers did not. It would have meant nothing to the Athenian philosophers if Paul had quoted and reasoned from an authority they didn't recognize. Paul met them where they were and used what they valued to show them something they did not. He started their journey toward Christ by speaking their language, leveraging the truth in their own sayings to point to the one true God.

This is not easy. But with practice and a commitment to learn, you

---

3. Paul contextualized two familiar Athenian sayings, presenting them in the light of the gospel. "In him we live and move and have our being" may have come from Epimenides of Crete (ca. 600 BC), and "We are his offspring" comes from the pagan poet Aratus (ca. 315–240 BC) *Phanomena 5*. See Darrell Bock, *Acts* (Grand Rapids, MI: Baker Academic, 2007), 568.

can do what Paul did. Paul was culturally savvy as a result of a life of learning. His unique influence in Athens wouldn't have been possible if he didn't know how the Athenian mind worked. And he quite obviously couldn't have used their poetry and philosophy against them had he not known it. You must commit yourself to growing in knowledge so you can be fruitful in the opportunities God may lay at your feet (Col. 1:9–10; 4:5–6).

Evangelism on Purpose

Some Christians think that using their minds undermines faith and having too much knowledge works against the power and leading of the Holy Spirit. But this is unbiblical. We are told to grow in knowledge, to plan, and to count costs. We are commanded to love God with our minds. This can be an act of worship. It can help us love others well, because the greatest way we can love this world is by helping them see what they most need—reconciliation with God. This was Paul's ministry, and it is our ministry (2 Cor. 5:18). Let us be good stewards. Let us prepare and plan to go, and let us make the most of every opportunity.

Chapter Fifteen

The Home

Daddy, why does God let people go hungry?
—MY DAUGHTER

The Danger in Talking to Five-Year-Olds

I was standing in the kitchen one morning and I thought I'd have some fun teasing my daughter. I know, Dad of the Year here. She asked for breakfast, and I said, "What? Mommy didn't tell you? We aren't eating breakfast anymore. We are only going to get two meals a day."

K.K. saw right through this and, with all the disdain a five-year-old can muster, said, "Daaaddy."

I smiled and then thought, I'll use this to teach her. "You know there are people in the world who only get one or two meals a day."

With amazement and shock she said, "Huh?"

"Yeah, a lot of people in the world are poor," I told her. "They don't have money to buy food."

It's fun to see how her five-year-old mind works. She immediately responded, "They must not have jobs and work hard."

I smiled. "No, some of them work very hard. They just live in places where life is much harder than where we live."

And here is why parenting is not for wimps. K.K.'s next question is the kind that makes you regret talking to five-year-olds. She said, "Why did God let that happen to them?"

Any suggestions on how to have a conversation about the problem of pain and evil with a five-year-old? How would you answer K.K.'s question? You must prepare yourself to be asked this and similar questions because your kids will ask them, and they will ask before you think they will.

Start Early

People often ask me how soon they should start apologetics with their children. My response: as soon as they start asking questions. The age when answers are meaningful is the age when questions are asked. Children are nearly always ready for more than we give them. Obviously, you can say more than a child can handle, but if you are prayerfully and gently pursuing the good of your family, teaching and answering questions starts at the beginning. If you wait until you think they are ready, it is already too late.

I don't wait. I engage. I answer questions and provoke them with questions of my own. And sometimes I make mistakes. Sometimes my answers introduce more confusion. Sometimes I back myself into a corner, realizing my children can't comprehend the answer yet. But this leads to funny stories, great memories, and a close bond with my children. They like to see Dad get tongue-tied. They like my silly analogies. They like to talk to me, and I like to talk to them. Open and ongoing communication is the best way to teach apologetics in the home.

When K.K. and I talked about the problem of pain, I did not give her a full answer. She is only a child. Part of my answer came from conversations we had already had. Answering your child's questions is an ongoing process. You cannot answer complex questions in one sitting, especially if you have no foundation for such conversations.

In our conversation about pain, K.K. actually answered her own question in part, based on our previous conversations. After I paused and thought about her question, I simply told her that bad is in the world because sin is in the world. She knows about sin: sin is all the bad things we have done that Jesus came to get rid of when He died on the cross. In her mind, Jesus died on the cross to get rid of all the bad. It may be a childish way to think—but she is a child, and her thinking is not wrong. While I was in the middle of explaining about bad being in the world because of sin, K.K. said, "Oh! And Jesus came to die on the cross and take away all the bad!" Then she smiled, gave me her storing information look, and then walked out of the kitchen content and satisfied knowing that bad exists because sins exists and that her good God has fixed it. He has a plan to end all the bad. Part of the plan has happened. Some of it is yet to come. But even five-year-olds know that not every good thing comes all at once.

Live Authentically

When you are trying to teach apologetics in your home, remember that the single greatest influence on the beliefs of children is the beliefs of their parents. Common sense and our own experiences show this to be true. More than anything in my life, the religious beliefs and practices of my parents influenced my beliefs. But research also shows this to be true.[1]

Children are learning sponges. They soak up everything around them. They are programmed to learn, and they learn first by watching. Your lifestyle is a powerful teacher. It shows them what is important. It shows them what is true. It shows them what you really believe.

---

1. Christian Smith, a sociologist out of Notre Dame, has been studying religion in adolescents for more than ten years. He and a team of researchers have found that an overwhelming majority (upwards of 70 percent) of young people have religious beliefs similar to their parents. See Christian Smith, *Soul Searching: The Religious and Spiritual Lives of American Teenagers* (New York: Oxford University Press, 2005), 35.

When children see active, authentic faith, they learn that God is of primary importance. They see the value of knowing and following Him. They see that He is not a component of life but the source of true life. However, when children see inactive, inauthentic faith, they learn that while religion may have some value, it is no more (and sometimes much less) important than sports or a hobby. It is something that might make your life better if and when it fits into your schedule.

By the time children can think abstractly, they have already learned through their parents the value of God and His place in our lives. This means that in the battle for the hearts and minds of children, the church cannot ignore the hearts and minds of parents. Church leaders must equip parents to know God rightly and follow Him faithfully if ministry to children has a chance at being effective. There is no such thing as a good children's ministry or youth ministry if there is no active ministry to parents. And, parents, take the responsibility—and privilege!—of growing up in Christ. Do not wait for the church to "feed you." Grow in knowledge and obedience, and your children will benefit because of it. Let your genuine holiness, your life of faith and obedience, be the first apologetic lesson for your families.

Provide Safety

Let me offer one more bit of practical advice. In addition to starting early and seeking righteousness, you must create a safe environment for honest dialogue. Your home is not the academy. Children should not feel the pressure of failure where they sleep. Teaching in the home can and should happen freely and opportunistically. But remember, you only seize opportunity when you are intentional about it, and you should intend to use every situation as an opportunity to teach your children (Deut. 6:7). But your ambition to teach will not be enough if your home is not a safe place to ask questions.

Much recent research has focused on the mass exodus of the

younger generations from religion. They are leaving the church in droves.[2] One of the recurring themes in the reasons young people provide for abandoning church is that they don't feel allowed to ask questions. Many have experienced or fear, "How could you think that?"—a response that implies you are either immoral or stupid for having the question. And nearly all have been shushed when asking a question, a response that implies both you and your question are worthless. Consequently, youth around the globe feel that they cannot express their doubts about their parents' and communities' core beliefs.[3]

This isn't anything new. Family tension has always existed. Parents have always been annoyed by pestering children's questions, and so they quickly silence them. There has always been pressure on younger generations to conform to the patterns of the older ones. The difference now is that, through the Internet, the younger generations have access to a wealth of other worldviews and an abundance of places to be heard. Previously, children had nowhere else to go with their questions if their parents put them off. Now, the world and its

2. "One-fifth of the U.S. public—and a third of adults under 30—are religiously unaffiliated today, the highest percentages ever in Pew Research Center polling." See "'Nones' on the Rise," *Pew Research Centers Religion Public Life Project RSS*, July 8, 2014, http://www.pewforum.org/2012/10/09/nones-on-the-rise/.

3. The idea that young people are unwilling to speak their minds may strike you as strange. You may think children and teenagers enjoy challenging the previous generation's beliefs. And you would be partially right. "Rebellion" is a normal part of moral development. It is the pushing of boundaries to see if they are real. It is the way children discover their autonomy and society's expectations. But youth do not rebel so that they will be considered "bad" by their community. Young people generally fear being an outsider. They fear having the dissenting opinion and not fitting in. And this is what they fear when they question religious beliefs. They fear being labeled as a bad kid, or worse, a kid that is going to hell. And so for a time, they adopt the religious beliefs of their community. And for some of them, the questions go away. But for others, unanswered questions create apathy toward God or even full-fledged rejection of Him.

views are at their fingertips. And somebody on the Internet is always willing to listen—and give an answer.

Children's questions today are more likely to go through search engines than their parents. Social media have greatly changed the way we relate to each other, and their greatest impact has been on the younger generation. Rather than go to a person who might judge you, get angry with you, or laugh at you, children and teenagers let the anonymous, lifeless World Wide Web teach them everything they need to know. Anyone can find a safe haven online where questions are embraced, encouraged, and answered.

But this need not be the case. Children, teenagers, and young adults alike would much rather have a person embrace them than their computer. But this will not happen unless you create a safe environment for honest dialogue. This is the starting place.

Then find reasons to connect with your children. Do not wait for them to come to you. This is an ever-changing task, because what children like to talk about is constantly evolving. But do not give up. Take an interest in what interests them, because it will give you their ear and convince them that they have yours.

My father did this with me. I went through a phase where heavy metal was my thing. So my dad listened to Metallica. During a period in my life when my foul music choices could easily cut me off from my parents, my dad made sure that did not happen. He entered my world so that he could hear me and talk to me.

Once your children start talking to you because they know you are listening, let them ask their full question. Often the first question is not the real question. It is a question to test the waters and see if it's okay to ask what's really on their mind. There is a reason the statement "there's no such thing as a stupid question" exists. We all have asked questions that we felt dumb about later, and we have learned that sometimes it's safer not to ask than to look stupid.

Questions reveal things about us. They tell others what we think about, including what we think of ourselves—our self-image. For adolescents, especially, the self-image is a fragile thing and some-thing to fiercely protect. Whether they realize it or not, they fight for it. Since asking questions makes them vulnerable, you must embrace questions, controlling your tone and expressions. When you embrace a question, you affirm the person. If people find their first question well received, they are more likely to ask another, and then another—until they get to the real question.[4]

The Front Line of Defense

Some people are talkers and some are not. I am the latter. Getting me to talk as a child was a bit like trying to pull my teeth out. But my home was a safe place and I knew it. I always felt there was an ear for my questions. I was never ridiculed for what I asked. The home my parents created gave me the freedom to ask questions. And in the freedom to ask comes the assurance that answers exist.

Silencing questions can make someone feel like something is wrong with them for asking such a thing or it can communicate that there is no answer to their question. We must never make a person feel bad because of a question they have. Jesus welcomed questioners and provided them with answers and reasons to believe.[5] We should too. And it should be easy for us to allow questions because we are on the side of truth. We have nothing to hide.

Your home can be the front line of defense. It must be. Our children need protection from the enemy's deceptive ways. Empty philosophy wants to take our children captive. You must always be on the look-out. Begin early, live authentically, and provide safety for your family so that they can find the truth and the freedom that comes with it.

---

4. Many of the insights in this section are a result of my time teaching at "The Campus" and my frequent conversations with its owner, Evelyn Plott.
5. Three examples of Jesus seeking to satisfy doubters are found in Matt. 9:1–8, John 11:1–27, and John 20:24–28.

Chapter Sixteen

The Church

Will I Have a Mustache in Heaven?
—LOCAL CHURCH BILLBOARD

Forsaking Wisdom

The church is known for many things these days, but, sadly, offering answers to life's important questions is not one of them. Many people in the church have abandoned loving God with their mind and only want to know Him with their heart—whatever that means. But you can't know God with your heart. You know Him with your mind. Only when the mind is filled with the knowledge of God and His wisdom can the heart love Him. Without knowledge, love is unfounded and empty.

The offering of empty emotion is part of the reason the church is becoming irrelevant in our society. You cannot experience God truly if you do not know Him rightly. But many churches are claiming to give people an experience with God, but they do not provide the knowledge necessary to do so. In a consumeristic society, they are overselling their product. They cannot deliver on this promise. As a result, there are plenty of people who think the church is nothing more than a bunch of charlatans, swindlers, and profiteers.

Solomon pleaded with his son not to despise wisdom but to seek it. His fatherly plea needs to be heard by the modern church. Wisdom sets the course of life. Finding wisdom takes work, but the true seeker will find it and be richer for it. But when wisdom is ignored, Solomon tells us it laughs at our calamity and mocks us when terror strikes (Prov. 1:20–33). Neutrality is not an option when it comes to wisdom: either you pursue it and reap the rewards or you neglect it and suffer the consequence. I fear the church has neglected it too long, and we are facing the calamitous results.

Prosperity easily breeds contempt for wisdom, and we live in a prosperous time. Christian consumers want a church that can meet their needs more than they want a community where they can learn and grow and serve. We want the church to feed us, serve us, and make us happy. We have become lazy gluttons. Instead of pursuing the knowledge of God, we pursue a version of Christianity that "works"—a religion that gives us the American dream rather than the kingdom of God. And the church has responded accordingly, catering to trends at the expense of giving people the truth they really need.

There was a time in American history when people outside the church took Christianity seriously. They assumed pastors had good answers. And it was not just because people didn't know any better back then. It was because many men and women of faith were intellectuals. They knew their Bible and their history. They could speak about theology and chemistry and literature. But today, many believers are ill-equipped to speak meaningfully about anything that does not have a mascot. Christianity has lost its voice in the culture because it has nothing of value to say.

Salt of the Earth and Light of the World

But this is not the kind of Christian the Bible portrays. Christians are heirs of the truth. We follow the One who created and sustains the earth. In Him is true wisdom and knowledge. We, of all people, should have something meaningful to say in the public exchange of ideas. God has given us to the world to be salt for its decay and light for its darkness (Matt. 5:13–16).

As salt, we are an essential ingredient in the recipe for a good world. We prevent moral decay, make life enjoyable, and help society be a better place. Part of our saltiness comes from a renewed mind, the mind of Christ. The world needs answers. We have access to them. It is that simple. Who else can offer words of life, words that lead to eternal life and words that cultivate life in the present?

The world needs serious Christians who are businesspeople and doctors and mathematicians and historians and mechanics at the top of their fields. The knowledge of God and His wisdom is valuable to everyone, and it is relevant to every area of life. Christians must let their light shine in all places. And the whole world will benefit because of it.

Imagine a world of lawyers and politicians who knew the Scripture as well as their professions. What if scientists were directed by biblical assumptions about life's origins? What if bankers and investors were guided by a Christian ethic? How would life improve? It is not only "ministers" who need to know God and His wisdom. We all do.

Not only does knowledge of God result in a general well-being for society, it spurs evangelism in the church. When Christians are confident in what they believe, they are passionate about sharing it. But many Christians lack a biblical worldview,[1] and an overwhelming number of them lack the ability to articulate their beliefs.[2] And so for

---

1. Less than 1 out of 5 born-again Christians have a biblical worldview. See "Barna Survey Examines Changes in Worldview Among Christians over the Past 13 Years," *Barna Group*, March 6, 2009, https://www.barna.org/barna -update/21-transformation/252-barna-survey-examines-changes-in-world view-among-christians-over-the-past-13-years#.VFl0TPnF-HA.

2. This is especially true of teenagers. See Christian Smith and Melinda Lund-

many it is an intimidating and even impossible idea to talk to others about God, someone they actually know very little about.

If the church is no longer very concerned about knowing God, the entire world will suffer. We must recapture and instill a desire for knowledge within the church.

Cultivating a Love for Knowledge in the Church

I am a pastor. Cultivating a love for knowledge in the church must begin with me. I must lead my church. I must challenge them in areas where they are uncomfortable. I must lead them into holiness. I must protect them from empty philosophy and deceit (Col. 2:1–8). I am a watchman. I am a servant. I must be faithful with what my master has placed in my charge.

But being faithful begins with understanding that my church needs more than knowledge. They need more than what I can offer from the pulpit. They need the warmth of fellowship that comes through healthy relationships. Moreover, I buy the right to speak truth by humbly submitting to my church. I am not above them. I live with them. This is where a love for knowledge of God begins in the church.

Knowledge can be a natural barrier between people. Knowledge often puffs us up and creates distance in relationships. If you want your church to love knowledge, you must love your church first. Serve your people: stack chairs, clean restrooms, go to recitals, send thank-you cards, remember birthdays, cry at funerals, and laugh at life.

Loving others demonstrates to them the true purpose of knowledge. Growing in knowledge is not just about learning the rules. It is not about being able to spout facts. It is about knowing God fully, such that you obey Him. And when you obey Him, you discover real life.

---

quist Denton, *Soul Searching: The Religious and Spiritual Lives of American Teenagers* (Oxford: Oxford University Press, 2005), 263.

An appreciation for knowledge does not come from a lecture or sermon. It comes through a relationship. When your church members see how the pursuit of knowledge has changed you for the better, they will want that knowledge for themselves. But if you use your knowledge to elevate yourself, people will despise you and run away from you. They must like you if they are going to listen to you. You might think, *people ought to listen to me because I know more than them!* But I trust people who I know are committed to me. Not just people who think they are smarter than me.

If you are a pastor, I urge you to take the lead. If you're not a pastor, let me help you serve your pastor. Understand that if your pastor seems to resist your desire to teach apologetics, he may not actually oppose the idea. It might be something as simple as bad timing on your part. When we are passionate about something, we expect the world to revolve around our passions. Many of you are passionate about apologetics. That is good. But your pastor's world does not spin around your sun.

Understand your pastor's burden. It is not easy to carry the load of three failing marriages, a son in jail, a mom with cancer, a staff member in sin, and a heretic all in the same church. Pastoring is a joy, and it is a pain. It is messy. It hurts. Your pastor carries the weight of others' burdens. Paul speaks of the struggle he faced for the churches he planted. He fought for them, he fought *with* them, and he suffered on their behalf. Your pastor does the same.

Let this knowledge season your approach to getting apologetics into your church. Remember that the church needs more than apologetics—and that is what your pastor is trying to provide. So if your pastor seems uninterested in listening to you talk about teaching apologetics, wait and try again another day. You may have simply caught him on a day when the sky was falling. Be patient. Don't pester him. And let him know you care about more than apologetics: you care about him and his family and you care about the church. Take your pastor to lunch. Mow his grass. Watch a ball game together. Join the nursery rotation. Chaperone a youth event. Be a greeter. Laugh together.[3]

If you want a pastor to use your gifts, he must trust you. And it takes more than your knowledge to earn the trust of your pastor. It will take your life. No one wants your knowledge if all it has done for you is make you proud and uncaring.

Persevere

I have had much experience with people who are uninterested in growing in knowledge. I've had people in my own church who see no need for apologetics. But I do not force it on them. I persevere in teaching and presenting opportunities to grow in knowledge, and I trust the Lord to work in their lives. One thing I have learned is that I don't always know what a person most needs. People are complex and there are always things in their lives that you don't know about. So when you encounter opposition to apologetics, be patient and persevere. Let me share a story to explain.

A gal in one of my former youth groups saw very little need to learn apologetics. Jennifer did receive a little training through a sermon here and a conference there. But for the most part she was uninterested. She had the opportunity to study apologetics for two years but never took advantage of it. Like many people in the church, she just didn't see the need.

Then one morning Jennifer walked into my office beaming. She could not wait to tell me about her "scary evangelistic meeting" during spring break. One day on the beach, a girl approached her and a friend to offer them drugs. When they politely but strongly declined, the girl asked why. Jennifer and her friend spent the next three hours talking to her about Jesus.

---

3. Twice now I have told you to laugh. Laughter fills my church. We enjoy each other's company. We tell jokes and pick on each other. If you want to have hard conversations, and you must have them in any family, you must also have light ones.

As they talked, the girl kept asking, "How do you know?" Every response Jennifer gave was met with "How do you know?" This can be a very intimidating question. Needing to back up your beliefs can make you feel like you're on trial. But much to Jennifer's surprise, she found it exciting because she realized that she actually had some answers. She also discovered that because she had answers she was more calm than the last time she shared her faith years earlier. Moreover, Jennifer could tell that the girl appreciated their gentle interaction. She appreciated that she could talk about God with Jennifer and her friend, rather than just be preached at. And she appreciated that someone had an answer besides, "Well, I just have faith."

I asked Jennifer how the talk ended. She beamed, "Great! I have her number. She lives in the next town over, believe it or not, and I am going to invite her to church. This sharing your faith thing is pretty fun." She is right. It is fun when you have answers. And this is what happens to people when they get a little knowledge in them. They turn into evangelists.

As Jennifer was walking back out of the office she said, "You know, that was pretty cool."

I said, "What was pretty cool?"

She replied, "Being able to give people answers to their questions." Then she looked past my shoulder and asked, "Do you have any books I could borrow that might help me with this?"

I smiled, walked over to my bookshelf, and helped her pick out a book. She gets it. She now understands the need for apologetics. She knows how useful it is in evangelism. And now she knows where to go to get more of it.

Slowly but surely, I've had more and more experience like this in my church. It has taken nearly three years. But take the time to do the little things that earn the trust of your church. Your job as an apologist is to gently but persistently stay in front of people with what you can do for them while you are serving them.

Someone once spoke these wise words to me: "What you have to offer meets a need. Be steadfast, keep it in front of them, and when they have that need, they will call on you." We want and expect immediate results. But this does not happen often. We must take a long view to integrate apologetics into our church. You cannot force people to know something. People seek knowledge because they love it, and they love it when it meets their needs. You cannot manipulate needs and you cannot force love. Sometimes all you can do is wait.

Many of us are in fields that require sowing. Some of us are in fields needing a harvest. Whatever your field, work the ground faithfully and humbly. Your desire to equip your church with knowledge is a good desire. It is one that meets a vital need. Keep what you have to offer in front of your people or your pastor, and when they recognize their need, they will call on you.

Epilogue

For I am not ashamed of the gospel, for it is the power of God
for salvation to everyone who believes, to the Jew first and
also to the Greek.

—ROMANS 1:16

As I end this book, let me encourage you to trust in the power of the gospel. Do not be ashamed to freely speak about the goodness of God's mercy and kindness. I have said before that most people reject God because of emotional and volitional issues. Intellect merely hides these issues. Though we have talked about evidence and logic and arguments, we must remember that the reason many people will not submit to God is their heart. But the loving-kindness of God's grace can soften a hardened heart and will draw many to Him.

All people recognize two things: there is a God and they have broken a standard of morality for which they should be judged (Rom. 1:18–2:16). All people struggle with guilt, and guilt is a powerful force that causes many people to run from God rather than to Him. Guilt often manifests itself in pride and the attempt to either rationalize sin or personally atone for it. Guilt sometimes results in depression, feelings of inadequacy, and the belief that no one should love them. Whatever it looks like, guilt is an obstacle to repentance.

But God is greater than our sin. His love is more powerful than our guilt. And His kindness will draw many to repentance. Don't place your hope in logic, history, science, and argumentation. Trust in the beauty of the gospel and God's mercy. Do not be ashamed of the gospel because it is the power of God for salvation (Rom. 1:16). Share it as often as you can.

The most overlooked part of apologetics is the gospel. Apologists tend never to get that far in conversations with nonbelievers. We sometimes think that people won't believe in the foolishness of the cross. So we resort to talking only about that which seems reasonable. But do not shy away from preaching what this world will consider foolish. Remember that apologetics is a servant of the gospel, and sometimes the servant just needs to get out of the master's way.

Christians, share the gospel with others, and tell them how God's grace has transformed you. You can offer the hope of a changed life. Tell your story. Explain what it's like to be forgiven. Talk about your anticipation of heaven. And joyfully speak about the peace of God that now fills your life.

Invite skeptics to meet God and enjoy all that comes from life in Christ. Feel the freedom to tell them that you know Him, that you've experienced Him, and that they can too. There is value in your experience and personal knowledge of God. Talk about it. Some people say that you cannot argue with a changed life, but you can; I argue with the good and changed Mormons all the time. But there is value in your conversion, in the reality that God can be known and experienced. So tell people your story and invite them to enter into one for themselves.

Questions for Personal Reflection and Small Group Study

Preface

1. Stop and think about the last time you shared your faith. What was that conversation like? What did you say? How did you act? What were your facial expressions? What was your motivation? What was the response? How did the conversation end? Now take a second to consider the time you shared your faith before that. Was it much different? If your conversations of faith are filled with much of the same frustration, emotions, and outcomes, ask yourself why.

2. What do you trust in when sharing your faith? Be honest. An easy way to answer this question is to ask yourself what keeps you from witnessing. If it is fear of not knowing an answer to a question, then you trust in your knowledge. If it is fear of rejection, then you place your trust in how others perceive you. Take a moment and write down what you think has the power to save someone and what keeps you from sharing your faith.

3. If the power of salvation is in the gospel (Rom. 1:16), what is the role of apologetics in evangelism?

Chapter 1: Holiness

1. What do you think of Brennan Manning's words at the beginning of this chapter? Have you had any experiences that relate to what he is saying?

2. What do you think causes people to live a "double life"? Why is it so hard to leave certain sins behind? What does it mean about your relationship with God when your life does not reflect His desire for how you should live?

3. Do you think that 1 Peter 1:15 is realistic? Why or why not?

4. Name one person whose life is a good reflection of their faith. How does their holy lifestyle affect the people around them? How does your lifestyle affect others?

Chapter 2: Humility

1. Have you ever "stretched" what you know to win an argument? Why did you do that? What was the result?

2. What could be some positive outcomes of admitting that you don't have an answer?

3. Read Philippians 2:3–8. How should these words from Paul affect how we share and defend our faith?

Chapter 3: Readiness

1. The older you get, the busier life becomes, and the faster time flies. Think about what consumes the majority of your time and thoughts. What do you worry about most? What are you most anxious about seeing happen? Where does sharing the gospel fit? How often do you feel burdened to proclaim the hope you have (Rom. 9:1–3)?

2. Read Matthew 5:14–16. What are some ways that your light shines before others? Have you ever had an experience where people have seen your good works and glorified your Father in heaven? Describe that experience.

3. Most Christians never think about why they believe, they just

believe. But to be ready to answer the question why you believe in something, you must think about it before it is asked. So, why do you place your hope in Jesus? Write down all the reasons for your faith in Jesus.

4. Being ready to share and defend your faith consists of having a pure heart and a prepared mind. Write down some practical ways to prepare each.

Chapter 4: Gentleness and Respect

1. Think of a time when someone told you that you were wrong. How did you feel? How do you typically react when someone tells you that you must change something about the way you live and think? As you think about those conversations, write down the things that make them go well or poorly.

2. We live in an age where respect equals full acceptance of both person and belief. Is this a correct belief? Why or why not? How is it possible to respect a person while holding that their lifestyle and beliefs are wrong?

3. Read Romans 5:1–11. Think of one person for whom you have no respect. Think about why you don't respect them. How should the gospel affect this situation? Write down some ways that the gospel can remedy it. (Be sure to think about how the gospel can help you as well!) Is there a way to love a person and not respect them?

4. What is the biggest thing that causes you to show a lack of gentleness and respect for another? Particularly in conversations of faith, what is it that makes you lose your cool? What can you do to remain calm in those situations?

Chapter 5: Listen

1. There are many reasons why we are unable to listen. Think about and write down some things that prevent you from listening well to others.

2. Like most things, listening is a skill that requires practice. How can developing a servant's mind-set help you in the skill of listening? What are some ways you can practice this?

3. This chapter says that most people read into comments more than they listen to them: "Often we put people and their beliefs in categories without really listening to them. Then we respond to the position or belief we think they have instead of trying to find out exactly what they believe and why." Is this true? Have you ever experienced anything like that?

4. How can asking questions help you listen? Take some time and think about some questions you can ask. Write them down and memorize them. This is one way you can practice listening even before you enter a conversation.

Chapter 6: Ask Questions

1. Children are great at asking questions that stump adults. Why is that? Why is it that a child's question leaves adults grasping for answers?

2. Explain the power of a good question. How does having the ability to ask a good question help when you share your faith?

3. They say there is no such thing as a "dumb" question and they are right. There are, however, many insensitive questions. Often questions display an ignorant bias or prejudice. Some questions are asked derogatorily. What are some bad questions you have asked or been asked when talking about your faith? What was the result?

4. A great way to prepare for defending your faith is to anticipate the questions others might ask you. Write down some questions that *you* have about your faith. Take some time to think about these questions.

Chapter 7: Stay on Topic

1. We live in an age where attention spans are short. How does this make sharing the gospel difficult?
2. Jesus said to be "wise as serpents and innocent as doves" (Matt. 10:16). How can staying on topic be an application of this teaching?
3. Staying on topic is a discipline that requires practice and strategic tools. One strategy is to write down the questions or arguments of the person with whom you are speaking. What is the value of stopping to write down questions and arguments in conversations about faith? What are some other practical ways to stay on topic?
4. Describe how listening and asking questions helps you stay on topic.

Chapter 8: Stick with What You Know

1. We all like to look smart. Often this means that we feel the need to answer every question or express our opinion. Sometimes this makes us talk about things we don't know much about as if we were experts. Think about a time you did this. Why did you do it? What was the result? What is the worst argument you have heard or given in the attempt to convince someone of Christianity?
2. Is there ever a time that it is okay to "stretch" what you know in order to win an argument about God or Christianity? Why or why not?
3. Don't bite off more than you can chew. How does this expression explain the principle of "burden of proof" (see pp. 65–66)?
4. What is the place of your knowledge when sharing your faith?

Chapter 9: Truth

1. What are some of the common beliefs about truth that you have heard? How would you define truth? Write the simplest definition of truth that you can.

2. What is relativism and why is it an enemy of the gospel?
3. How would you respond to the person who claims that absolute truth does not exist? Write down your response.
4. How does theism provide justification for a belief in human rights?
5. How can a person's moral outrage be used to leverage the gospel?

Chapter 10: God

1. What are some of the most frequently asked questions you hear about God? What are some of your questions? Is it okay to question God's existence or His goodness? Are doubts and questions a sign of a lack of faith? Write down your responses and discuss them in your group.
2. What are some ways that God has made Himself known? What are some ways that God has made Himself known to you personally? Which of these help you the most when doubts creep in? What do Romans 1:18–23 and 2:14–15 have to say to this?
3. This chapter says, "Most people's objections to God are not intellectual; they are either emotional or volitional. It is not so much their mind but their heart that rejects God." If this is true, what implications does it have for presenting evidence for God's existence?
4. How can evidence for the resurrection of Jesus answer many of the questions that skeptics ask about God? Write down your answers and then talk as a group about ways to steer conversations toward the cross.

Chapter 11: Religion

1. What is religious pluralism? Explain its contradictory nature.
2. Some would grant the position that God exists but claim that people are incapable of knowing Him. They would say, as Thomas Paine did in *The Age of Reason*, that religions are merely "human inventions, set up to terrify and enslave mankind, and

monopolize power and profit."[1] How would you respond to this claim in light of all of the examples of corruption and violence associated with religion?

3. Do other religions contain truth in their teachings? If so, what does this mean for the exclusive claim of John 14:6?

4. What are some specific challenges to sharing the gospel with people of other religions?

Chapter 12: Scripture

1. This chapter says, "Strictly speaking, the fate of the Bible is not related to the fate of God. You cannot dismiss the Bible and think that will get rid of God." What is the strategy behind this statement? Do you think it is effective? Why or why not?

2. Most people haven't studied the Bible or its reliability. They just don't believe it. Why do you suppose people are so quick to dismiss the Bible?

3. Most people would be surprised to learn about the incredible reliability of the Bible. What information provided in this chapter was the most interesting to you? What information do you think nonbelievers would find most compelling? Discuss this as a group and consider ways to help people understand the reliability of the Bible.

4. Write a short statement describing the reliability of the Bible.

Chapter 13: Evil and the Problem of Pain

1. What is the most important thing to remember and focus on when discussing the problem of evil and pain?

2. Think about how the problem of evil and pain has affected you. How did you wrestle with God's goodness in the midst of a tragedy? What gave your heart rest? What questions do you still have

---

1. Thomas Paine, *The Age of Reason*, part 1, section 1, 1793–94, public domain.

about this topic? Write these things down and discuss them with your group.

3. This chapter claims that the problem of pain is a problem for skeptics because the existence of evil is proof for God's existence. Do you agree? Why or why not?

4. Read Romans 3:21–26. What does this passage show us about God's justice?

Chapter 14: The World

1. What are some things that keep you from *going*?

2. If actions are the results of beliefs, what does our lack of evangelism say about our beliefs?

3. Give a simple definition of Paul's method of evangelism.

4. What do you need to be effective in evangelism?

5. Where are places you could go to connect naturally with people?

Chapter 15: The Home

1. Think about your home growing up. How did your family influence you and your beliefs about God?

2. If the greatest influence on the religious beliefs of children is the religious beliefs of parents, what are some practical applications of this truth? How should we respond?

3. What are the three components of teaching apologetics in the home described in this chapter?

4. Many children and teenagers do not have parents who seek God and so will not teach their children the ways of the Lord. How can we serve them?

Chapter 16: The Church

1. What has been your experience with apologetics in the church? Why do you suppose so many people and pastors seem opposed to teaching apologetics?

2. How can apologetics serve the church?

3. What role should the church serve in society? How does cultivating a love of learning within the church affect its role?
4. How is faith misunderstood? What is the right understanding of faith and how does it relate to knowledge?
5. What are some practical ways to grow personally in knowledge?
6. What are some ways to pour love into your church as you seek to pour knowledge into it?

Epilogue

1. Write down the story of your redemption. How were you saved? What convinced you?
2. What obstacles stood in your path to forgiveness?
3. A person's heart is the primary reason for unbelief. How can your personal testimony help others come to Christ?
4. There is value in telling people about your personal experiences with God. I encouraged you to invite people to experience God for themselves; but I also said that I will argue with Mormons about their experiences with God. Is this contradictory? Discuss the role that your experiences with God should play in your personal evangelism.
5. Jot down some of the ways the Lord has used this study to strengthen your faith, satisfy your heart, and equip you for sharing the gospel.

Topical Resource List

I HAVE ENCOURAGED you throughout this book to study further. Here is a list of resources arranged thematically. This is not an exclusive list; these books are not the only ones worth reading on a given topic. But I have listed some of the books that have helped me, and I hope they help you. The titles in **bold** are the ones I suggest you read if you read only one from each section. I also suggest you read C. S. Lewis's *Mere Christianity* before you read any of the others.

Abortion

Beckwith, Francis J. *Defending Life: A Moral and Legal Case against Abortion Choice.* New York: Cambridge University Press, 2007.

Francis Beckwith has written an in-depth and comprehensive book on abortion. At times it can be a hard read, but it is rich in insight and practical applications for the abortion discussion.

Rae, Scott B. *Moral Choices: An Introduction to Ethics*. 3rd ed. Grand Rapids: Zondervan, 2009.

Scott Rae's *Moral Choices* is a great book on a host of ethical issues. Included is a very good chapter on abortion, perhaps the best treatment of the abortion issue consolidated into a single chapter.

Doubt

Habermas, Gary R. *Dealing with Doubt.* Chicago: Moody Press, 1990.
———. *The Thomas Factor: Using Your Doubts to Draw Closer to God.* Nashville: Broadman & Holman, 1999.

Gary Habermas has done perhaps the best work on the subject of doubt. He has also done the world a favor by making *Dealing with Doubt* and *The Thomas Factor* available for free at http://www.gary habermas.com/books/books.htm.

Lewis, C. S. *A Grief Observed.* San Francisco: Harper San Francisco, 2001.

C. S. Lewis addresses the issue of doubt in *A Grief Observed,* which is about the loss of his wife. This is a very personal book, and you get to see very intimately how Lewis handled the doubts that he faced in the loss of his wife.

Ethics / Morality

Rae, Scott B. *Moral Choices: An Introduction to Ethics.* 3rd ed. Grand Rapids: Zondervan, 2009.

Rae's book *Moral Choices* is a must-read. It is a comprehensive and readable study on ethics and ethical issues faced by the modern Christian. It can easily be used as a textbook. High school students and adults alike will benefit from this book.

Evil / Pain

Lewis, C. S. *A Grief Observed* and *The Problem of Pain.* San Francisco: Harper San Francisco, 2001.

A Grief Observed and *The Problem of Pain* both deal with the difficulty that the existence of evil presents to Christianity. *A Grief Observed* addresses the issue of pain in a very intimate and personal way as it is a book about Lewis's struggles in the loss of his wife. *The Problem of Pain* is a more philosophical look at the issue of evil and pain. I would recommend you read them both. If you are hurting, read *A Grief Observed* first; if not, read *The Problem of Pain* first.

Plantinga, Alvin. *God, Freedom, and Evil.* Grand Rapids: Eerdmans, 1977.

Plantinga is often quoted and referenced. A well-respected Christian philosopher, he takes a philosophical and logical approach to the problem of evil. This book is for the person who likes logic and needs to explain the problem of pain to a friend who is a student of logic. That is not to say that you should not read it; I am just letting you know what to expect.

General

Craig, William Lane. *Reasonable Faith: Christian Truth and Apologetics.* 3rd ed. Wheaton, IL: Crossway Books, 2008.

It is said that Craig has never lost a debate. He is a brilliant man. *Reasonable Faith* is a brilliant book, but it is one that you will need to spend time with. It is not for the novice apologetics reader. But if you are committed to studying apologetics, this is a book that you should read. It presents very strong and detailed arguments for God's existence, making much use of science, history, and philosophy along the way.

Dembski, William A., and Michael R. Licona. *Evidence for God: 50 Arguments for Faith from the Bible, History, Philosophy, and Science.* Grand Rapids: Baker Books, 2010.

This is a collection of fifty essays from various writers who provide arguments for the Christian faith. Each essay is direct and to the point. The chapters can be read in less than five minutes each, and it is a great resource to get a general view of virtually every argument for God and Christianity.

Flew, Antony. *There Is a God: How the World's Most Notorious Atheist Changed His Mind.* New York: Harper One, 2008.

At one time Antony Flew was regarded as the world's most influential philosophical atheist. He changed his position before he died. To my knowledge he did not become a Christian, nor hold to any other religion, but this book is an interesting read to see his spiritual development.

Geisler, Norman L. *Baker Encyclopedia of Christian Apologetics.* Grand Rapids: Baker Books, 1999.

This book is exactly what it says it is, an encyclopedia of apologetics. A good addition to your library for quick reference and hard-to-find facts, it covers virtually every apologetic topic.

Geisler, Norman L., and Frank Turek. *I Don't Have Enough Faith to Be an Atheist.* Wheaton, IL: Crossway Books, 2004.

Turek and Geisler team up to write this fantastic book on the evidence for the Christian faith. It is written with you in mind. It goes in-depth, but is not wordy. It teaches more than it philosophizes and is a must-read as it presents a very good comprehensive argument for the Christian faith.

Geisler, Norman L., and Ronald M. Brooks. *When Skeptics Ask: A Handbook on Christian Evidences.* Revised and updated. Grand Rapids: Baker Books, 2013.

This book is a good resource for quick reference on common questions skeptics ask. It is written in a way that makes the content easily understood.

Lewis, C. S. *Mere Christianity*. San Francisco: Harper SanFrancisco, 2001.

Mere Christianity is perhaps my favorite book of all time. It covers much in apologetics and is written in a way that can be understood and enjoyed by all. Lewis's wit and wisdom have changed many lives. *Mere Christianity* is a collection of his wisdom regarding the validity of Christianity. Spend time with it and you will be rewarded.

Moreland, J. P. *Love Your God with All Your Mind: The Role of Reason in the Life of the Soul.* Revised and updated. Colorado Springs, CO: NavPress, 2012.

We live in an age when too much emphasis has been placed on experiencing God to the exclusion of knowing Him. Moreland's book calls for Christians to recapture an intellectual life. It is a must-read and will help the church experience God more truly, as well as recapture a position of influence within society.

Implementing Apologetics

Baucham, Voddie, Jr. *The Ever-Loving Truth: Can Faith Thrive in a Post-Christian Culture?* Nashville: Broadman & Holman, 2004.

Baucham shows how today's Christians face problems similar to those of first-century Christians. He argues that we live in a post-Christian culture similar to their pre-Christian culture and shows how we can engage our culture as our predecessors did.

Koukl, Gregory. *Tactics: A Game Plan for Discussing Your Christian Convictions.* Grand Rapids: Zondervan, 2009.

This book changed the way I talk with skeptics. Recently, I was at a conference where Koukl spoke, and after Koukl was finished, my friend turned to me and said, "I see where you learned what you learned." This book is very practical and will equip you to engage skeptics in meaningful, respectful, and fruitful conversations.

Kreeft, Peter. *Socrates Meets Jesus: History's Great Questioner Confronts the Claims of Christ.* Downers Grove, IL: InterVarsity Press, 2002.

———. *Between Heaven and Hell: A Dialog Somewhere Beyond Death with John F. Kennedy, C. S. Lewis and Aldous Huxley.* Expanded, 2nd ed. Downers Grove, IL: InterVarsity, 2008.

Works of fiction, these entertaining books contain conversations about apologetic and philosophical issues. Through Kreeft's characters, the reader sees different ways to talk about apologetic issues. These books are a different way to learn about apologetics and to see how to use what you know.

Zacharias, Ravi, and Norman Geisler. *Is Your Church Ready?: Motivating Leaders to Live an Apologetic Life.* Grand Rapids: Zondervan, 2003.

This is a collection of essays a bout implementing apologetics in your church. It is a must-read for church leaders who desire to equip their people to spread the gospel.

Miracles

Geivett, R. Douglas, and Gary R. Habermas, eds. *In Defense of Miracles: A Comprehensive Case for God's Action in History.* Downers Grove, IL: InterVarsity Press, 1997.

Geivett and Habermas serve as general editors in this collection of essays that argue for the possibility and identification of miracles. The various essays create a comprehensive defense against skeptical objections to miracles as well as set forth a positive case for God's action in history. This is a good read and virtually all people could benefit from reading it.

Resurrection of Jesus

Copan, Paul, and Ronald K. Tacelli, eds. *Jesus' Resurrection: Fact or Figment?: A Debate between William Lane Craig & Gerd Lüdemann.* Downers Grove, IL: InterVarsity Press, 2009.

Watching and reading debates are great ways to learn how to talk to skeptics and how to answer their questions. This book includes the

Craig-Lüdemann debate along with follow-up essays that offer additional information on the resurrection. Also included is a critique of both men's arguments.

Flew, Antony. *There Is a God: How the World's Most Notorious Atheist Changed His Mind.* New York: HarperOne, 2008.

This book is not about the resurrection; it is about Flew's abandonment of atheism for deism. However, at the end of the book there is an appendix written by N. T. Wright, per Flew's request, on the resurrection. Though Flew did not hold to any particular religion, he recognized that Christianity is the one religion that should be honored and respected. Furthermore, he thought that the claims of the resurrection were more impressive than any other religious competition.

Habermas, Gary R., and Michael R. Licona. *The Case for the Resurrection of Jesus.* **Grand Rapids: Kregel, 2004.**

Gary Habermas and Mike Licona teamed up to write perhaps the best book available of the historical evidence for the resurrection of Jesus. Using only evidence that is agreed upon by secular and religious historians alike, Habermas and Licona show that the best interpretation of the historical data is that Jesus rose from the dead. This book is well written, intended for a broad audience, and is certainly worth your time. It even comes with an interactive computer game to help you retain what you read.

Science

Rana, Fazale. *The Cell's Design: How Chemistry Reveals the Creator's Artistry.* **Grand Rapids: Baker Books, 2008.**

Biochemists have made startling discoveries in recent years about the complexity of the cell. In this book, Rana explores the scientific and theological impact of these discoveries and shows how the cell is evidence of an intelligent designer. Intelligent design is one of the strongest arguments for God's existence and this book will help you, particularly when sharing your faith with those of a scientific mind.

Wells, Jonathan. *Icons of Evolution: Science or Myth? Why Much of What We Teach About Evolution Is Wrong.* Washington, DC: Regnery, 2002.

Wells, who has a PhD in molecular and cellular biology from the University of California at Berkeley and another PhD in religious studies from Yale University, explains how much of what is being taught about evolution is wrong. He gives examples of blatant misrepresentations and factual errors in textbooks. This book is good if you are dealing with a person who is hardened against God because of a strong belief in evolution.

Truth

Kreeft, Peter. *A Refutation of Moral Relativism: Interviews with an Absolutist.* San Francisco: Ignatius Press, 1999.

This work of fiction addresses moral relativism by way of conversations between two characters. It is an enjoyable way to read about the absurdity of moral relativism, and it provides tips for speaking with relativists yourself.

World Religion / Worldviews

Corduan, Winfried. *Neighboring Faiths: A Christian Introduction to World Religions.* Downers Grove, IL: InterVarsity Press, 1998.

We live in a diverse culture, and it is good to know about the different religions in this culture. Evangelism is more profitable when we know the people we are talking with, and Corduan's book is a helpful resource for those who need a general introduction to the major world religions.

Geisler, Norman L., and William D. Watkins. *Worlds Apart: A Handbook on World Views.* 2nd ed. Eugene, OR: Wipf and Stock Publishers, 2003.

Worldviews are like colored glasses; they affect the way we see the world. It is very helpful to understand how a person's beliefs cause them to think in particular ways, and it makes witnessing to them more effective because it enables you to communicate the gospel more clearly.

Rhodes, Ron. *The Challenge of the Cults and New Religions: The Essential Guide to Their History, Their Doctrine, and Our Response.* Grand Rapids: Zondervan, 2013.

In our diverse culture, you may at some point meet someone who has been involved in or influenced by a cult and its teachings. Rhodes's book does a very good job of explaining the nature of cults, the different teachings of particular cults, and appropriate ways to respond to them.